D1456455

innervation

INNOVATE COUNTS.

WHERE IT INSIDE.

innervation

redesign yourself for a smarter future

Guy Browning

PERSEUS
PUBLISHING

A Member of the
Perseus Books Group

www.yourmomentum.com/innervation

the stuff that drives you

What is momentum?

Momentum is a completely new publishing philosophy, in print and online, dedicated to giving you more of the information, inspiration and drive to enhance who you are, what you do, and how you do it.

Fusing the changing forces of work, life and technology, momentum will give you the bright stuff for a brighter future and set you on the way to being all you can be.

Who needs momentum?

Momentum is for people who want to make things happen in their career and their life, who want to work at something they enjoy and that's worthy of their talent and their time.

Momentum people have values and principles, and question who they are, what they do, and who for. Wherever they work, they want to feel proud of what they do. And they are hungry for information, stimulation, ideas and answers. ...

Momentum online

Visit *www.yourmomentum.com* to be part of the talent community. Here you'll find a full listing of current and future books, an archive of articles by momentum authors, sample chapters and self-assessment tools. While you're there, post your work-life questions to our momentum coaches and sign up to receive free newsletters with even more stuff to drive you.

More momentum

If you need more drive for your life, try one of these titles, all published under the momentum label:

change activist
make big things happen fast
Carmel McConnell

lead yourself
be where others will follow
Mick Cope

happy mondays
put the pleasure back into work
Richard Reeves

the big difference
life works when you choose it
Nicola Phillips

snap, crackle or stop
change your career and make your own destiny
Barbara Quinn

float you
how to capitalize on your talent
Carmel McConnell & Mick Cope

coach yourself
make real change in your life
Anthony M. Grant & Jane Greene

grow your human capital
what you know, who you know, how you use it
Hilarie Owen

Many of the designations used by manufacturers and sellers to distinguish their products are claimed as trademarks. Where those designations appear in this book, and where Perseus Publishing was aware of a trademark claim, the designations have been printed in initial capital letters.

This edition of *Innervation: redesign yourself for a smarter future* First Edition is published by arrangement with Pearson Education Limited.

Library of Congress Control Number: 2002116173
ISBN 0-7382-0660-1

Perseus Publishing is a member of the Perseus Books Group.
Find us on the World Wide Web at http://www.perseuspublishing.com.
Perseus Publishing books are available at special discounts for bulk purchases in the U.S. by corporations, institutions, and other organizations. For more information, please contact the Special Markets Department at the Perseus Books Group, 11 Cambridge Center, Cambridge, MA 02142, or call (800) 255-1514 or (617) 252-5298, or e-mail j.mccrary@perseusbooks.com.

Concept design by Heat
Production design by Claire Brodmann Book Designs, Lichfield, Staffs

First printing, February 2003

1 2 3 4 5 6 7 8 9 10–06 05 04 03

Thank you....

for buying this book or simulating enormous pleasure if you got it as a present.

I'd also like to thank Fiona McAnena, Ed McCabe, Graeme Wilkinson, Brian Jenner, Katharine Viner, Clive Digby-Jones, Rufus Olins and Rachael Stock. Without them the intellectual content of this book would have been pitifully thin.

And, finally, a big thank you to Esther and Cecilia for getting me up in good time to write it.

opening

three big assumptions about you

the future is arriving so fast you may already have missed it

being

thinking

doing

opening

innervation

momentum

three big assumptions about you

This book is based on three biggish assumptions about you.

1 You want to make good things happen

This book is for those people who are trying to make things happen, who want to be part of the solution and who are looking for ways of working better and living a fuller life.

There are three kinds of people in the world; those who make things happen; those who watch things happen; and those who wonder what happened.

Jack Welch, CEO, General Electric

I'm not sure Jack was the person who said this, but in business the rule is if you don't know who said it, say Jack Welch said it. Nobody's going to argue.

2 You want to balance life and work

The quality of life and work are inextricably intertwined. This book assumes you have decided that you are not just going to live to work, nor are you just going to work to live – you're going to try to get both right.

The quality of a person's life is in direct proportion to their commitment to excellence, regardless of their chosen field of endeavour.

Jack Welch possibly?

3 You can think for yourself

If all the answers were easy, you'd already know them. None of the answers, suggestions or thoughts in this book are off-the-shelf solutions with guaranteed results. They worked for me and for the examples I give but you must use your own judgement about everything you read.

Please don't sit back and put your brain into neutral. Select permanent four-wheel drive and continually question everything you read. It's more than likely that I've got something wrong, I've missed something or I'm just talking through the back of my pants.

One of the biggest lessons everyone has to learn in the new economy is that it's up to you – more and more things are your choice, your decision and your responsibility. You've got to take information on board and then decide for yourself whether it's got any value and whether it should be acted on.

You can't teach a man anything, you can only help him discover it within himself.

Galileo (if not him then see above)

There would be no point finishing this book and saying, 'Guy Browning is the solution to all my problems'. For this book to succeed, you should put it down and say, 'I am the solution to all my problems'. (Preferably after you've read it.)

the future is arriving so fast you may already have missed it

The new economy – what is it?

For the last century or so, technology has been mass producing products, jobs and human beings. In the new economy, you're on your own. You choose what you want to do, how you want to do it, and who you want to do it with. Now is the age of mass individualization – millions of different people with millions of different choices and with the freedom and prosperity to make them. No one can tell you what to do.

A lot of the froth has blown away from the new economy. E-commerce is no longer seen as El Dorado. Millionaires are not being made overnight. Far more significantly, there are vast changes in the way individuals work and do business that have already happened and will continue to happen, driven by new technology.

Perhaps the most important consequence of the technological revolution is the speed of information transfer. In other words, more people know more things more quickly. For the customer it means they can shop around, negotiate and purchase in seconds. We're not just talking about book buyers here, we're talking about how major industrial and commercial organizations run their businesses. We're also talking about how individuals and small groups of individuals organize their work.

Broader access to up-to-date, top-quality and far-reaching information means that the traditional building blocks of business and undemocratic governments, such as hierarchy, monopolies and command and control management, are all increasingly undermined.

As the technology improves and all the various formats converge, consumers will stop noticing the technology and focus ever more closely on the content. That's why marketing will be the dominant commercial skill in future. Not the old-style advertising, PR, long-lunching style of marketing, but all the skills required to establish an immediate rapport with your markets and to develop a symbiotic, trusting relationship with them.

When information and choice proliferate, certain features assume more importance: clarity, simplicity, and attractiveness. First impressions will become more important than ever because people won't have the time to get to know you or your offering. On the other hand, if people decide they like you, they have the ability to ask you all the searching questions. And if they don't like what they see, then they know that the Internet will present them with another choice in seconds.

In the same way, relationships in the workplace will have to become more symbiotic and trusting because workers in the knowledge economy know that their next job is a click away. Ironically, the net result of so much intensive technological development and change is that the human face of business will become far more important.

I've seen the future and I don't recognize it

When you look at the future of business one thing is absolutely crystal clear. But nobody knows what that thing is. However, there are some predictions we can make with complete confidence.

Communication

In the near future you can make a pretty safe assumption that everyone will have a mobile phone and access to the Internet. There will be more and better ways of communicating but we will continue to ignore all of these and keep people in the dark until something goes disastrously wrong.

Having more means of communication is like getting married and acquiring a load of in-laws. The possibilities of communication are increased but it doesn't mean you talk to any of them.

Working environment

The other thing that will happen is that offices will become more like home and home will become more like the office. Offices will get more and more cozy with trendy cafés, soft furnishings, casual clothing, crèches and pastel shades, while an increasing part of home is taken up with files, computers, faxes and desks. Eventually people will be desperate to get to work, where they can drop off their kids, sink into some soft furnishings, get some decent food and generally be treated more like a human being.

Increasingly, everywhere that isn't home or work will become a combination of the two. Hairdressers, car showrooms, station waiting rooms, supermarkets and banks will all become relaxing, friendly environments that you can work in, or feel at home in, or both. You'll know you're in this kind of space, because you'll be able to smell coffee.

Bosses

Bosses will disappear. When everyone's working from home, nobody's going to volunteer to have a boss in the spare room. To all intents and purposes everyone will be their own boss. Bosses will become people who have the skills to co-ordinate the activities of lots of individuals, i.e., people who can communicate well. Generally, good communicators are people who listen rather than talk so we'll all have bosses who listen to us rather than the other way round. The downside of this is that we'll have to think of something worth saying.

Big business

Big businesses will continue to get bigger and more global in their reach. But working for them will be very different. You'll spend less time in the office and more time working from a plane and from home. People in big businesses will be required to work more quickly than ever before, in smaller, more flexible teams. Working for a big company will require all the same skills as working for yourself.

Small business

An increasing amount of business will be done by individuals and small bands of people linking up to tackle the task in hand, and then moving on to the next task and a new team. Outsourcing and insourcing will be replaced by prosourcing or picking the appropriate team for every individual job whether they come from outside or inside the business.

Products, services and brands

As information becomes more widely available, technical product differentiation will become increasingly difficult. Competitive advantage will become a function of affection for the brand and will therefore be driven by product excellence (a given), brand awareness and loyalty, design, and marketing. Widespread information will also make consumers increasingly aware of the processes behind the brand and the ethical stance of the company. The ethical dimension of brands will be an increasing factor in brand loyalty – in other words how your values and the values of a brand interrelate.

What does it all mean for you?

In some important ways, the Internet has led to globalization, especially in the sharing of information, ideas and culture. The other perhaps unintended result has been localization. From your armchair you can find out the menu in your local pub and the name of the landlord. The Internet is not only creating a global village, it's also recreating the traditional local village.

The *mind* of the Internet is globalization in that it is a forum for the unlimited exchange of ideas. But the *heart and soul* of the Internet is putting real people in touch with each other in real places. Because in the real world you always trust what's nearest to you.

Globally and locally everyone will increasingly know everyone else's business. And there's no better check on behavior than being in the spotlight. In the new economy the spotlight is on you and your business. It's time to rewire yourself for the new economy and reassess who you want to be, how you think about things and what you want to do in life.

Working people are now in a game without rules, in a world without frontiers, in organizations so flat you can see all the way to the horizon.

And everything is on fast forward. You're now head to head with a new business reality. How quickly can you listen, learn, adapt, attack?

You're now on your own. Forget hierarchies, processes and systems. Ditch any notion of becoming a jetsetting, highrolling, pinstriped corporate soldier ant. Nobody likes them or the way they do business. The new economy needs a new kind of person. Personal innovation – **innervation** – is the new skill for anyone who wants a future in business. It's about how to imagine and build businesses, teams, networks, relationships and fulfilling lives. It's about a new and more complete way of **Being**, **Thinking** and **Doing**.

Most of all it's about challenging and rebuilding the one thing you DO have total control over – yourself. It's time to delayer yourself, rightsize your ego and vertically integrate your entire life.

Look on your brain as the Internet

If this book were a website you probably wouldn't have started at the beginning. You might choose to start at page 80. Why not? It's a very good page if you don't mind me saying. Books are one of the last things in this hypertext, super-accelerated, parallel processing world that we start at the beginning and work our way through to the end.

OK, life starts at the beginning and finishes at the end but what's happened to all the stuff in the middle? School, job, marriage, kids, retirement, death. Not any more. How about job, retirement, kids, learning, marriage, death. You can do them in just about any order you want these days, although death still seems to claim the last laugh.

Internet protocol (IP) is a system by which data, whether it's voice or otherwise, is divided up into lots of little parcels of information that are then dispatched on the Internet. All the little parcels take the fastest route available to them and then reassemble themselves when they arrive at the other end. IP is the future of communication whatever the medium.

It's also remarkably similar to the way the brain works. The brain, like the Internet, is composed of billions of different connections. The information we receive from our senses is composed of little parcels of data that find a billion different ways of navigating through the brain before they become a coherent thought.

Most of us use our brains in the same way we use the post. We get our little piece of information and send it down the same old delivery network until it arrives safe and sound. It's slow, but it's reliable and best of all it's nice and safe and familiar. With this style of thinking we get the same old information, in the same old format, which we process in the same old way and, not surprisingly, we get the same old thoughts.

This isn't good enough for people who want to work and succeed in the new economy. In fact it isn't good enough for anybody who wants to think differently, benefit from a plethora of experiences and generally suck the marrow from life.

We have to learn to treat our brain like the Internet. We have to be open to a universe of new inspiration and experiences wherever they are found. We need to have the courage, open-mindedness and practical techniques to be able to search our brains and experiences for new thoughts and perspectives. We need to have a million different ways for routing our thinking (or a lot more than one at least).

The brain is a creature of habit. It likes to process things efficiently and if this means thinking and doing things like it has in the past then it's happy to keep on doing it in that way. Given its head (as it were) your brain would be quite happy being 95 per cent idle. But we're not going to let it.

This book is going to show you how to rewire your brain, your outlook, your thought processes and perhaps even your entire life.

It's about innovating where it counts most – *inside*. Because external breakthroughs, changes, ideas all start from within.

So let's get started with the most interesting, difficult, complex and potentially powerful thing in your universe. **You**.

The old new economy

At the close of the last century there were two easy ways of making money in Britain. One was to have a distant ancestor who came across with William the Conqueror a thousand years ago and stole a large chunk of the country. The other method was to become a dotcom millionaire.

Becoming an internet millionaire was very simple. Firstly, you took the name of a household object, such as egg, plug, dog, then you added a .com after it. You didn't need an idea, an office, any staff or even any idea of how you were going to make a profit. However, it did help if you were good looking, wore trendy clothes and were very young – under 30 was good, under 20 was excellent, under 10 a definite bonus.

And of course, the younger you were the less experience you had in real business, and that was also very good. You didn't need experience on the Internet because you didn't need to make any money. You just said you were going to sell shares in your company, and lots of older people with no ideas and boring clothes would give you their money.

The next morning you woke up and found that you were worth more than most traditional heavy industries built up over hundreds of years. It was vital that you then had a press conference at which you wore your trendiest clothes and told everyone that the money really wasn't important to you. You tried not to laugh as you said this.

If you wanted to stay a millionaire there was a critical moment just after everyone had given you their money and just before everyone realized that you didn't have an idea, office, profit, etc. That was the time to sell your shares and take up farming. Sadly, 16-year-old computer millionaires were too young and too inexperienced to do this and they ended up losing all their money and becoming 17-year-old poor students, just like everyone else. That meant they had to go to work driving delivery vans. There were lots of these van-driving jobs around because people increasingly liked to buy things like food and books on the Internet that were then delivered to them at home.

Everyone thought it was fantastic that you could order your weekly shopping on the Internet instead of spending hours at the supermarket or stuck in traffic. So, instead, they spent hours at home waiting for the delivery van that was stuck in traffic. And what did they do while they were waiting? They played on their computer and suddenly had a great idea for an Internet business that would make them a million.

being

get ahead by being a bastard (and waste your life doing it)

How to get ahead by being a bastard

Some of you reading this may already be bastards and I apologize if I'm teaching you to suck eggs. It's more than likely that you aren't a bastard or you don't know that you are one. Bastards who know they're bastards don't spend a lot of time on self-improvement.

Everyone has worked for or with someone who they consider rude, unprincipled and downright unpleasant. What's equally galling is that many of these people do exceptionally well in business. This is for two reasons:

◆ most importantly, traditional command and control hierarchical businesses encouraged that sort of behavior as long as the right results were forthcoming;

◆ bastards tend to promote and encourage people who behave like they do, i.e., other bastards.

I realize that 'bastard' is not a technical description for these people and one person's bastard is another person's best friend in all the world. The people who I'm talking about are people who use selfish, bullying, underhand and mendacious tactics for getting their job done and getting ahead.

It's interesting to see how these people operate, if only for historical reasons. There's no mystery to how they work and if you want to go down that route here's what you have to do.

Talk loudest and don't listen to other people

Getting your needs across to other people is paramount. Talk loudly at people and force them to hear what you're saying. Don't waste time listening to them. They'll only want help doing something or make excuses for not doing what you want. Communication works where it is loud and long and doesn't encourage a lot of backchat.

Don't help anybody else do anything

Helping other people involves time and energy which could be better spent on your own projects. There will always be people who need help. God helps those who help themselves.

Over-promise and under-deliver

It's very easy to take people for a ride once because on the whole people are very trusting. You can take their hard-earned cash from them by promising all sorts of things and then you can rip them off. Nothing illegal of course, just substantially under-deliver on what you promised. You can do this with goods, services and personal relationships. Remember, there's one born every minute so you're never going to run out of potential people to exploit.

Lie and then lie about lying

Lying about things saves all sorts of trouble and most people tend to give you the benefit of the doubt. If anyone accuses you of lying, say it was all a misunderstanding and apologize. You won't mean either of course. If you're going to lie in the first place, you're certainly not going to start telling the truth to your accusers. Remember that lies always travel quicker than the truth so you can always stay one step ahead.

being

innervation

momentum

Talk behind others' backs

It's an information economy so spend some time spreading your own information. All truth is subjective so your version of events and analysis of people is as likely to be as accurate as any other. If someone's going to turn their back on you, then why not use it as a knife rack.

Take the credit for others' efforts

People are working so hard they really won't mind if you take the credit. After all, if you've given them the work to do in the first place, surely you should take the credit for it – they wouldn't be doing it if it weren't for you. This is especially the case for good ideas – who's to say who had an idea first? It occurred to you seconds before someone told you, didn't it? Just because they said it first, doesn't mean they had it first. And anyway, possession is nine-tenths of the law.

Bully people weaker than you are

It's amazing how much you can get done by shouting at people, abusing them, belittling them and generally making them feel scared and small. If they were right about something they'd fight back, wouldn't they. Anyway they're just wasting time for the most part and if they can't stick up for themselves they're probably not very interesting.

Waste other people's time

Your time is more important than other people's time. Arrive for meetings when you're ready. Give people really tight deadlines so that you've got more time. If they're so fussy about time they won't mind. Also, don't deliver when you promise. If they really want something, they won't mind waiting.

Concentrate on money and power

What else is there? If you've got more money and power than someone else, then you're clearly a better person than they are and it's important you make them aware of this by following all of the above rules.

In life you get what you give. The bastard misreads this as you get what you get.

Because they never grasp this rule they never wake up to the wider truth that you've only got one life to live and if you spend it doing ugly, shoddy things to people, it will all add up to an ugly, shoddy life.

You don't have to wait until the last judgement to know whether or not you've done something ugly and shoddy. There's no escaping it because when you go to bed, you know exactly how shoddy you've been to others in life. You don't need anyone to tell you. It's your life and your choice and no amount of alcohol, drugs or anything else will disguise this fact from you.

Thank you for that, O Great Prophet

That's a pretty biblical note to start off a book on the new economy but it's important for two reasons:

◆ Because business in the real world has really unpleasant people doing really unpleasant things. Unless you understand how they behave, why they behave like they do, and the business consequences, the alternative forms of behavior are just going to seem like a lot of white-toothed, wishful thinking.

◆ Behaving like a bastard is becoming as increasingly redundant in business as Latin is as a business language.

Once again the new economy changes the rules.

In the new economy nobody will be obliged to take orders from anyone else.

There won't be pyramid structures of bosses and bosses' bosses. Nor will you get stuck with suppliers or business partners you don't like or respect. If you don't like doing business with an individual you won't have to because you'll have a thousand other choices.

That's sounds pretty utopian, I know. But technology will remorselessly strip away the layers from arrogance, bullying and lies.

being

innervation

momentum

As an individual, as a company, as a political party, you will have to be seen to be doing the right thing in the right way or you will be found out and then you will be history. The big irony is that soulless technology will lead to a more ethical way of doing business.

How to manage bastards

Bastards, like wasps, reproduce. As long as people work and live together there will always be people who you would prefer not to work or live with. Inevitably, even in the new economy, there will be times when you have to deal with them. Here's how you go about it.

Ideally avoid them

When you sniff out a bad apple, the best way of dealing with it is to throw it away. Or, if you're not in a position to do any throwing, move yourself as far as possible away from the bad apple. Remember, unless you're in prison, you can always leave.

Don't threaten them

Contrary to most impressions, bastards are usually insecure about something and their behavior is a symptom that they are damaged in some way. This doesn't make them any less dangerous but it does mean that you can avoid provoking them if you have some understanding of what they feel threatened by.

There is a vast range of what people feel inadequate and threatened by: looks, education, accent, height, race, creativity, background, family, clothing, humor, intelligence, women, men, speed, groups, efficiency, individuals, sales, meetings, presentations, etc., etc., etc.

Get to know their bosses

People who bully by virtue of their rank are usually pathetically submissive when it comes to people who outrank them. If you can get to know their managers and open a direct channel of communication with them, you have a good line of defense (and attack).

Make your work above reproach

This is more difficult than it sounds. Firstly, getting your work above reproach in normal circumstances is hard enough, let alone doing it with a bastard around. Secondly, if someone is determined to pick holes in your work, they'll find a way of doing it. But don't make it easy for them.

Get what they say in writing

Bastards ask you to do things and then blame you for doing them. They then blame you for not doing things they specifically asked you not to do. They'll do this anyway, but if you get their instructions in writing, they'll have to think twice before countermanding their own instructions.

Stay calm always

Bastards win when you lose control. Never show that they've hurt you in any way or that anything they say or do affects you emotionally. Bastards feel powerful when they think they have power over your feelings. Extreme politeness is the best armor when you're with them. Cry when you get home.

Manage them proactively

When you know you're working with a bastard you need to anticipate trouble: you need to check instructions, double check information and triple check intentions. Bastards are at their most dastardly when they're trying to get out of a corner. If you can manage business so they're never in a corner, you'll mitigate their worst behavior.

Develop a support network

There will always be others who recognize the bastard for what he really is and who suffer as you do. Use them to help you manage the bastard and reduce the impact of his attacks. They're also great for moral support.

Anticipate trouble

Bastards will always probe for weakness before they attack. It's better to strike back early and to give a clear signal that you're not to be messed with.

being

innervation

momentum

This will reduce the likelihood of further attacks. Remember to give regular reminders that you're not to be messed with.

Choose how you react

Bullies operate on the principle that you will react firstly with fear and secondly by doing what they say. But remember, however bad things get, you always have the freedom to choose how you will react to them and their intentions.

Reaction options

- Leave
- Accept
- Reject
- Debate
- Negotiate
- Delay
- Argue
- Compromise
- Listen
- Respond
- Right

- Ignore
- Support
- Offer help
- Seek assistance
- Acknowledge
- Shout
- Develop
- Review
- Champion
- Agree
- Disagree

- Avoid
- Embrace
- Nod
- Divide into sections
- Answer truthfully
- Change the subject
- Jump in
- Step back
- Laugh
- Cry

- Allocate resource
- Check timing
- Influence
- Distribute work
- Carry out instructions
- Mutiny
- Panic
- Act calmly
- Control
- Citizen's arrest

Attack only with overwhelming force

Once in a while a bastard has to be tackled head on. Sometimes a straightforward confrontation will bring them crashing down because, at heart, most bullies are cowards. However, many bastards are also hard bastards who will fight viciously to protect their position. If you have no other option but to attack, then attack with overwhelming force, with great speed and make sure they are completely defeated. A wounded bull is more dangerous than a normal, unpleasant bull.

How to manage bastards

◆ Ideally avoid them

◆ Don't threaten them

◆ Get to know their bosses

◆ Make your work above reproach

◆ Get what they say in writing

◆ Stay calm always

◆ Manage them proactively

◆ Develop a support network

◆ Anticipate trouble

◆ Choose how you react

◆ Attack only with overwhelming force

Being a bastard lesson 1: mess about with other people's time

In every corporate statement of values there is something about respecting other people's time. Similarly, in every organization there are people who respect other people's time so much they insist on using up as much of it as possible. The worst offenders are people who always arrive late for meetings.

Many men in business measure their masculinity in terms of how late they can be for a meeting. For them, arriving on time would show you were extremely junior or that you had so much free time you could afford to sit around waiting for other people to show up. Being late to a meeting shows everybody attending it just how little time you've got and how lucky they are to have someone so in demand at their meeting. This largely explains why a meeting that starts on time is as rare as understatement in the marketing department.

There is a finely graded scale of lateness for a meeting. Anything between five and ten minutes doesn't really count because that time is taken up pouring the coffee and swapping notes on how bad the traffic is. Twenty minutes late is the entry level for serious latecomers, with half an hour to really impress. Anything over half an hour risks people not waiting, so latecomers usually manage to turn up after about 25 minutes.

Behavior on arrival will demonstrate where an individual is in the office hierarchy. Lower orders will shuffle in timidly and then sit there like a lemon understanding absolutely nothing because they missed the crucial bit about why everyone's there. Other boss-like people will breeze in and start pontificating about a subject that has actually been covered in the first ten minutes. (Anything that has been agreed before they arrive will need to be unagreed on principle in order that their input is recognized as vital in the decision-making process.)

Latecomers always shake their head in a bewildered way and let out a great sigh as though their lateness was the result of some cosmic conspiracy against them rather than the fatness of their heads. Strangely, were there to be a meeting at which promotions were being given out on a first-come, first-served basis, those very same people would be at the front of the line.

It's very difficult to combat this kind of perpetual lateness among bosses because it stems from a form of intoxication, generally with the sound of their own voices. The only solution is not to invite them to the meeting in the first place. Sadly, this isn't normally possible as most meetings are actually called by bosses to lecture everyone on team work and mutual respect.

Being a bastard lesson 2: how to be sorry and not mean it

Apologies are the old rubber tires hung over the sides of huge egos to prevent damage when they rub up against each other. Apologies are all the rage these days. If you can't stomach an apology you can just say you regret something. This is shorthand for 'I regret being in a situation where an apology is called for'. In fact, modern apologies don't mean that you apologize, you regret anything or you are at fault. They're just the most polite way you can say, 'I dislike you intensely.'

An apology can be short-term pain for long-term gain. An apology, played right, can actually give you the upper hand. Firstly, you've shown that you're big enough to admit you're wrong. Secondly, you've obviously had to take the pain so you are in some way the victim and they are the brutal oppressor even though they're right on some slim technical grounds.

From this position you can either counter attack: 'I've said I'm sorry, what do you want, Blood!?' Or you can play the self-flagellation card: 'I'm wrong, I'm always wrong, I'm a worthless human being.' Or there's the philosophical approach: 'Factually you're right but in moral terms I'm right.'

A breezy apology can be very annoying. Quickly saying, 'I'm sorry, what an idiot I am', denies the other person the chance to say, 'Apologize, you idiot.' Never repeat the fault in the apology: 'I'm sorry I called you a grumpy old trout and I want everyone here to know that.' If you're really sorry you can send a huge bunch of flowers and a little note saying, 'I'm sorry I made fun of your pollen allergy.'

Apologizing on behalf of other people is also a good tactic. Try arriving late at a meeting and saying, 'I'm sorry you all arrived early.' Expert apologizers apologize even when it's obvious they're absolutely right. This gives the impression not that they're sorry but that they're sorry for you, for being such a loser.

The only time it's really easy to say sorry is when saying sorry simply isn't enough. 'I'm sorry I blew your leg off' doesn't really do it. What's called for is a lifetime of remorse. And you can't just say, 'I've blown your leg off, I can feel a lifetime of remorse coming on.' You've got to feel it, live it and show it, even though deep in your heart you know it was really their leg at fault.

Being a bastard lesson 3: how to be right all the time

Some people think that the easiest way to be right is to do and say absolutely nothing. The trouble is, the day before you die, you realize you've got your whole life wrong. Another method of always being right is to live slightly behind the event horizon so that you can be permanently wise after the event.

Others never admit to being wrong even though all the evidence screams that they are. They're still right because conditions weren't right for them to be right and had all the facts been utterly different they would have been totally right.

On the other hand, it's no good being completely right about something nobody gives a monkey's about. Nobody cares that you're completely right about the height of a gasometer.

If you're going to be right about everything (and it's astonishing how many people are), the simplest way is to decide from the outset that being wrong is not an option for you. Once you've got this settled, you develop two attendant medical conditions, jaundiced eye and sieve ear, which combine to give the impression that everything in life supports whatever you decide is right.

If you don't have the head of a pig, an easier way to be right is to have infinitely flexible opinions so that you can start a sentence with one opinion and finish it with another. However, if you don't have firm opinions you forsake the pleasure of saying, 'I told you so' or 'You really cacked that one up, Bernie.'

Being right all the time isn't easy, as right and wrong keep changing. For example, it is now right to wear corduroy trousers. That doesn't mean you were right to wear them non-stop for the last 20 years in the teeth of opposition from friends, family and fashion editors.

Don't ever try to prove someone who's always right, wrong. Even when you think you've done it, 30 years later they'll call you out of the blue and tell you that they were right about that gasometer all along.

The reason the final judgment is such an appealing idea to many is that those who live with the always-right expect them to be proved wrong and those who are always right expect to have this confirmed. The final judgement will decide once and for all who is right. Unless of course they get it wrong.

being

innervation

momentum

do the right thing (and be happy doing it)

Happy people at work

There is a small but irritatingly persistent group of people in the office who enjoy their work. They consume work like normal people consume chocolate and treat themselves to special little extra projects that involve doing more lovely work.

Office happy people seem to have some sort of invisible stress-proof coating. Stress doesn't exist for these people because when you give them something to do with a shocking deadline they smile sweetly and produce a beautifully bound report that they prepared earlier that week because it was something that really interested them. People who love their work seem to find it easier to do than normal people. They always seem to know about a button on the computer that saves five hours' work and lets them go home early with a song in their heart.

Happy people don't have people problems in the office or if they do they don't take them very seriously. They get on with everybody and everybody gets on with them. They're interested in what other people think but not in what they think of them.

Occasionally, through some malicious twist of fate, these happy, smiling people lose their jobs. Naturally this doesn't make them unhappy. Three months later, when they're in a job with new found heights of contentment, they'll tell you that losing their previous job was the best thing that could have happened to them.

How do these people do it? What is the secret of being happy?

How to be happy

Happiness is like a scooter; once you're up and running, you can just scoot along. It's getting up in the first place that's the tricky bit. Happiness needs to be kick started and the secret of doing this is to stop the brain worrying. Left to its own devices, the brain likes to prove how intelligent it is by being miserable. Have you noticed how intellectuals tend to be glum because it looks so much cleverer than walking around whistling like the village idiot.

Happiness is all about forgetting yourself and realizing that, despite everything, it's a beautiful world out there. (Don't confuse forgetting yourself with forgetting things, because if you rush out into the beautiful world and forget your keys, you're not going to be happy for very long.)

For example, meeting up with a party of like-minded women to sort out three tonnes of copper collected for charity will be a laborious job and will get your hands very dirty but, halfway through, when everyone's working away and the jokes about spending a penny are flowing thick and fast, a lovely feeling will set it. That's happiness.

Being busy doing something constructive is the fastest way to happiness because it keeps you and your mind occupied.

Music is the food of happiness: if you catch yourself whistling, humming or singing to yourself, you are happy. The best workout for making yourself happy is to sing songs in the bath at high volume because filling your lungs full of air is also a short cut to happiness. Miserable people don't like breathing; they smoke, slump around and mumble. If they were to stand up straight, take big breaths, speak

being

immervation

momentum

clearly and exercise regularly they would be very happy. They wouldn't have any friends but, boy, would they be happy.

One of the drawbacks of being happy and knowing it is that you feel an urge to clap your hands. Never reply, 'I'm very happy,' when someone asks you how you are, as it gives the impression that you are one step away from madness, religious conversion or both. Virtually all behavior associated with happiness such as whooping, skipping, hugging and whistling is frowned upon in public unless it's been induced by alcohol.

The only way you can be sure someone is happy is that they make you feel happy too. Unhappy people, on the other hand, tend to make other people unhappy often to prove just how unhappy they really are themselves. Happiness is quietly infectious – it's the virus that dare not speak its name.

That's lovely but we need clear instructions for this happiness business

Ask most unhappy people why they are unhappy and it generally boils down to the fact that they haven't got what they want. The first step to happiness is therefore to have a clear idea of what's important to you and what will make you happy.

It's not easy to assess your own life, so to give yourself a bit of objectivity look on yourself as a brand. (There are lots of business books on *You as a Brand* if this approach takes your fancy.)

Opposite is a list of how to build a brand that any good marketing person would agree with. If you don't agree with it, clearly you're not a very good marketing person.

Now put yourself through the process as if you were a brand.

Clearly define brand values

What's life all about for you? Do you want marriage, children, your own business, a wide circle of friends, a lot of money, exotic travel, excitement.?

> **How to build a strong brand**
>
> ◆ Clearly define brand values
>
> ◆ Communicate brand definition to all
>
> ◆ Rigorous quality control for product
>
> ◆ Build functional and emotional benefits
>
> ◆ Brand every detail of delivery
>
> ◆ Be consistent in brand communication
>
> ◆ Jealously guard brand equities
>
> ◆ Train the people who deliver the brand
>
> ◆ Constantly nurture affection for the brand
>
> ◆ Continual evolution not revolution

You need to define what you want out of life, what you value and what your values are. Once you're clear in your own mind about this you're more likely to achieve it.

Communicate brand definition to all

Once you've defined what's important in life there's no point in keeping it to yourself. If you've decided marriage is important to you then you need to get out there and get amongst marriageable material. If you want to earn more money, then make sure you're in a high-paid job and ask for what you want.

Rigorous quality control for product

If something is worth doing, it's worth doing properly. That applies as much to conducting a romance as it does to building a riveting robot. The Cub Scouts have a phrase for it: 'We will do our best.' Very occasionally, your best may not be good enough in the circumstances, but if you know you've given it your best shot, that's all that counts.

Build functional and emotional benefits

What are the advantages to people of living and working with you? What is it they like about you? You don't have to be all things to all people, but you can make sure that you have some aspects that people value you for: reliability, generosity, creativity, understanding, IT expertise, etc. To feel valued for something is a key to happiness.

Brand every detail of delivery

Do your own thing in your own way. People will accept you for what you are and see through you if you try to be something you are not. Besides which, you'll only really be comfortable doing things your own way. Many people spend their entire twenties discovering what their own way is, and their thirties doing it, so don't worry if you're not clear about your identity yet.

Be consistent in brand communication

Treat all people and situations equally. Don't be one person to one friend and a different one to another. You'll only end up confusing them and yourself.

Jealously guard brand equities

Look after yourself. You're all you've got. Don't let other people ride roughshod over what's dear to you, whether that's your loved ones, your career aspirations or your dreams.

Train the people who deliver the brand

You are the person who delivers your brand. Never stop learning and that includes learning about your nearest and dearest as well as acquiring new skills for work.

Constantly nurture affection for the brand

Relationships with family, friends and workmates need continual attention and servicing. The more you put into relationships, the more you will get out of them. Taking someone for granted is the surest way to lose them.

Continual evolution not revolution

Life is continually changing and you have to change with it. There are few challenges we can't cope with if we take them one step at a time. Massive revolutionary change should only be tried if all else has failed.

Follow these steps and you'll end up a well-rounded, well-balanced, well-adjusted individual. But what happens if you're starting from a very weak position indeed. What if you see yourself as a cheap brand with unattractive packaging that people only deal with because they have to?

How to stop being miserable

It's very difficult to start being happy when you're not happy, especially if you're actually downright miserable, even bordering on the depressed. There are some days, many of them in February, where everything is so miserable and depressing that you can feel all your energy, confidence and self-respect disappearing over the horizon with its ass on fire. You then have a choice: either you can immediately book yourself a four-month holiday in the Caribbean or, if that's not possible for some reason, you can pull yourself together.

The difficulty is that when you're feeling glum the last thing you want to do is to pull yourself anywhere. The only thing you want to pull is the phone out of the wall, the top off a bottle of gin and the duvet over your head. To be honest, nothing, apart from powerful hallucinogenic drugs, will have you laughing and skipping with happiness overnight. To start being happy, you have to stop being miserable although you should be aware there's a significant time lag between the two.

being

innervation

momentum

The secret is to treat yourself like an ailing business.

You need to take control of yourself, cut out the dead wood, prune yourself back for new growth and generally give yourself new structure, discipline and motivation.

Oddly, when you're feeling low the first instinct is to do the exact opposite, in other words a whole range of things that immediately make you feel worse:

◆ you sleep with someone 90 per cent unsuitable for the 10 per cent comfort factor;

◆ you go shopping for clothes which are 90 per cent overpriced and 10 per cent suitable;

◆ then you eat a catering tub of ice cream which makes you feel 90 per cent sick and 10 per cent depressed;

◆ you then don't go to a party because you feel so miserable and then you wonder why nobody phones you (they're all at the party).

Emergency de-glumming program

Firstly, get moving. Take your dog for a walk that's so long it thinks it's auditioning for a remake of *Incredible Journey*. If you don't have a dog, walk to somewhere you usually drive to and back. Or if that's too daunting go to the gym and test your sneakers to destruction.

Then, when you get in, put a load of washing on, make something large and hot to eat, wash up all your dirty dishes, tidy up the whole house, throw lots of old things away, pour yourself a large drink and then look through your photo album to remind you of the good times. (Don't do this if you generally look like a dork in photos.) Have another large drink, put your favorite CD on at an unethically high volume and then dance around like an idiot until you collapse with exhaustion.

And finally, when you get into bed, remember however bad things are, they're a lot worse in other parts of the world. Except in the Caribbean, of course.

When you feel glum you think that the world is an awful place, that everything in it is conspiring against you and that never has one person suffered so much. When you next feel like that, try standing in front of a mirror and saying to yourself: 'The world is an awful place, everything in it is conspiring against me and never has one person suffered so much as I have.' Not many people can do this and keep a straight face because you just look sorry for yourself. Alternatively, if you can say it and mean it, or if things are so bad you can't bear the sight of the mirror, you need to put yourself through the emergency de-glumming program.

How to be relaxed about stress

Once you have decided to get a grip on yourself you need to tackle the source of your unhappiness. Personal relationships aside, the biggest cause of unhappiness is stress arising from work and the people with whom you work. Follow these rules to reduce stress to a minimum.

Stick to your own agenda

Stress almost always comes when you're doing something for someone else. People who are working extremely hard on projects that they love don't suffer stress. Generally, if you can stick to work that meets your own agenda and in which you can see a direct benefit to yourself, you will reduce stress.

If it's not necessary, don't do it

At work, a lot of time and energy is spent doing things that don't need to be done. Either these tasks are unnecessary for the job in hand, or they are too much for the job in hand or the job in hand is actually completely unnecessary. The rule is to think before you start – is this really necessary and would my time be better spent doing something else entirely?

Say thank you, but no thank you

This is the key to reducing stress. When you're asked to do something that is not on your own agenda or seems completely unnecessary, then the easiest way to avoid stress is to say a polite 'no'. It's the easiest way to avoid stress but it's also one of the most difficult things to say. People are naturally obliging and it takes strength and confidence to say 'no'. When you can though, it's hugely liberating. Often saying 'no' is a great negotiating position from which you can offer limited and efficient assistance that won't stress you out.

Simplify everything you do

Over-complication is the breeding ground for stress. When there are too many people involved or too many tasks or too many targets, stress proliferates and you spend more time managing the problem than solving the problem. Before you start on a problem or situation, cut it down to its bare bones. Decide what is vital to the situation, what is just wallpaper. Get to the nub and then tackle that. Everything else will fall into place.

Get ahead and stay ahead

One of the main causes of stress is lack of time to complete work and one of the main reasons for having no time is that people either have too much work to do or they have fallen behind time. The more you fall behind, the worse things get until eventually you break down. The trick is to get ahead and stay ahead so that you always have the confidence of knowing that there is extra time if you need it. Get into the habit of starting work as soon as you get it and finishing it before deadlines. Even when you think you've finished a project before a deadline, it's amazing how many extra little improvements you can fit into the remaining time.

Never take your work home

The definition of a workaholic is someone whose desire to work is stronger than his desire to go home. That's why people who work from home tend to be more efficient because they can never slip off home early. Many workaholics are actually homeaphobics – people who are afraid of going home. They spend all their life slaving away to pay the mortgage on a house they'll only ever see in the dark.

Once you start taking your work home, you start to erode your family life. Work should be finished at work (even if this means the room upstairs) and left at work. Unless something desperate is happening at work, your family have more important things to talk about.

Jealously guard your time and space

The more helpful you are in life the more people will ask for your help. However, you will very quickly stop being of any help to anyone if you can't manage your time and space. There is a saying that if you want something done quickly, ask a busy person. Why? Because they're used to doing lots of things quickly and will be able to manage another task efficiently. Having said this, managing your own agenda first is paramount. Unless you're on top of your own work, you won't be any help with anybody else's. Get used to putting time in your diary for things you need and want to do.

Relax your body and your mind will follow

Stress affects the body and there are all sorts of unpleasant stress-related illnesses such as backache, viruses, skins diseases, plague, etc. On the other hand, looking after your body can help reduce stress. A good run, swim, bike ride or mammoth sex session after a hard day at the office can put it all in perspective and make you feel much more relaxed.

Laugh, eat well, enjoy company

Stressed people can forget that life should be enjoyed. Even when you're under time pressure you shouldn't start scrubbing out lunches, drinks and other social occasions from your diary. Extra time spent worrying about the job won't be as productive as extra time not thinking about the job at all.

Relax, it's only a job

When you're really under the gun it's worth taking a deep breath and reminding yourself that it's not Bosnia. Nobody is going to die or get hurt.

being

innervation

momentum

There are other jobs out there, and the welfare state if you're desperate. And whatever unpleasantness you're currently in the middle of, one thing is absolutely guaranteed – sooner or later it will be over.

How to be relaxed about stress

◆ Stick to your own agenda

◆ If it's not necessary, don't do it

◆ Say thank you, but no thank you

◆ Simplify everything you do

◆ Get ahead and stay ahead

◆ Never take your work home

◆ Jealously guard your time and space

◆ Relax your body and your mind will follow

◆ Laugh, eat well, enjoy company

◆ Relax, it's only a job

How to change your life

Any fool can chuck in his job, sell his house and sail off to the six continents. However, you're not really changing your life, you're just chucking in your job, selling your house and sailing to the six continents. A much more profound change is having grapefruit for breakfast. Inviting fruit into your life, especially at breakfast when you're at your weakest, is a much more difficult challenge, especially if you decide to wave goodbye to your sausages at the same time.

Changing what you wear can also completely change your life. For example, if you've spent the last ten years in thick corduroy trousers and then decide to go out and buy a pair of cargo pants, you're suddenly going to feel very uncomfortable with folk music.

Dramatic haircuts in both men and women are often an outward and visible sign of an inward and spiritual shift. In reverse, you can often trigger a shift in outlook by changing your hair style: for example, give yourself a side parting and notice how your shoes begin to look smarter and how the urge to pull your socks up intensifies.

If you regularly disagree with someone, try agreeing with them for a while. This is extremely unnerving for them and also gives you the moral high ground, which is a lovely place with great views. Changing partners is a good way of changing your life but should be approached with care. Partners, like underpants, should only be changed when not to change them becomes absolutely unthinkable.

Every night half the population look through the TV listings and say that there's nothing on. The other half think it's TV heaven. Swap halves. Once you get into the stride of changing your life it takes on its own momentum. Not only are you on a different train to work but you're reading bits of the paper that you've never noticed before.

Now, of course many of us are creatures of habit. We know exactly what we like and we make sure we stay well inside our comfort zone. Just remember that there's always somewhere more comfortable than your comfort zone and eventually that thought will make you so uncomfortable you'll venture out.

Or, you may not. You may in fact have your life so well-ordered that you don't want to do or change anything. Technically, however, you're not actually living and, if your heart and mind were linked to a monitor, you'd be flatlining. So unless you quite like the sound of being part of the living dead, reach for the grapefruit.

being

innervation

momentum

never hit a jellyfish with a spade

How do I do the right thing when I don't know what the right thing is?

If you're going to make a success of life in the new economy and be happy at the same time, you're going to have to decide what is important to you in life. In the same way as there are no longer any career paths, there are no longer any clear life paths.

Ideally, you want to avoid the situation whereby understanding what you want in life is a death bed revelation. Most of us have a very rough idea of what we want from life and what's important to us in terms of the way we get it. We want to look after our families, have a measure of career satisfaction and try to be nice to others along the way. (I may just have stumbled on the meaning of life there.) What most of us don't have is a very clear moral code to guide us in all life's major decisions and experiences.

Historically, the moral underpinning of Western civilization has supposedly been the ten commandments. Very few of us know what the ten commandments are; indeed, very few ministers and priests know what the ten commandments are. We all just about remember something about doing unto others, not killing people and there's something about an ox in there somewhere.

When it becomes interesting is when you ask a group of business people to write a new set of commandments for the 21st century. This is an exercise I often do with groups in order to get them focused on the ethical dimension of a problem. I've made a top ten list of what the groups have come up with in the past.

The new ten commandments

1 Treat other people as they want to be treated

2 Be generous with your time and talents

3 Respect other people's culture and beliefs

4 Don't discriminate on race, gender or sexual orientation

5 Look after the environment

6 Listen

7 Respect other people's time

8 Tell the truth

9 Put something back into the community

10 Love and protect your family

One interesting variation concerns number 1 on the list which, of course, is the golden rule from the original ten commandments. The expression of this varies between 'treat other people as you want to be treated', and 'treat other people as they would like to be treated'. This is not just a matter of a few words being slightly different but actually has serious consequences in business and in society at large.

When organizations are accused of being 'institutionally racist' it's not to say that everyone in that organization is a racist, it's more a reflection of the fact that the institution treats other people the way it would like to be treated itself. In a multicultural society, the way a predominantly white organization would like to be treated itself is not necessarily the same as the way people from other ethnic or cultural backgrounds would like to be treated.

Similarly, you may think you know how customers would like to be treated but how they want to be treated may be something entirely different. And of course this rule applies to your relationships with everybody including your nearest and dearest.

Just because you like sleeping with the light on doesn't mean they do.

The lesson from this is *never* to assume you know what people want. First you have to ask them, then you have to listen to them, understand them and adapt your behavior accordingly.

The new commandments in the new economy

With a few changes in words, the above list could easily be the value statements of any one of a number of large multinational companies and it's interesting that it falls to businesses today to set some moral markers in the ground to which they promise to adhere. This is actually a reflection of the fact that consumers increasingly want transparency in the companies they deal with. They want to be sure not only that the companies produce the right things but that they also produce them in the right way, i.e., without the improvement of dangerous chemicals, child labor, oppressive regimes, etc.

In the future, there will be an increasing number of businesses and organizations focused around a particular moral approach to a problem whether this is in cosmetics, transportation, food production, healthcare or fashion. Businesses are beginning to crystallize in their value statements what they deem to be the consensus moral opinion of their entire consumer base which goes across nations and across cultures. This brings us right back to the individual and her moral outlook. It's up to you to decide how you want to live your life, and from that certain choices will evolve.

How to be good

Feeling good about yourself helps you to be happy. If you behave badly, you're going to feel bad. But nobody tells you how to be good any more. Why not? Because nobody thinks it's their responsibility, because people think that goodness is relative and because being good sounds incredibly boring.

That's not very helpful, especially when you're engaged in a hard business practice like designing the way a call center will interact with customers. I've asked many different groups in business to think about what it means to be good on a daily basis and there is broad agreement on what it takes to be good and why.

Listen

When you're listening to other people you're not focusing on yourself. You're also better able to communicate with other people, get along with them and support them. No amount of talking will make up for not listening. Listen, and learn, and understand. Sounds pretty simple, listening. But why do you think that there are so many helplines for people in trouble of one kind or another? Because what they need in the first instance is always someone who will listen to them.

Be generous with your talents

Everyone has some kind of talent whether it's the brain of a genius or a strong pair of arms. Use your talent to help other people as well as yourself. You'll feel better about yourself and others will feel better about you and admire rather than envy your talents.

Don't speak ill of the living

Criticizing people is a deeply satisfying thing to do because, let's face it, other people are a pain in the neck. We all do it and no doubt lots of people do it behind our backs. Criticizing people is harder to give up than smoking. Like smoking, whining with someone about someone else is a great way of bonding. Also, like smoking, talking down people eventually messes you up inside.

The reason you criticize someone is always because something they do provokes a reaction in you that you can't completely manage. Nobody complains about people who do things that provoke manageable or pleasant reactions. Instead of criticizing people, see how you can change your response to them so that what they do doesn't fill you with negative thoughts about them.

I realize that what I've just said needs the patience and self-control of a saint. We don't want to give up whining and gossiping as they're just too much fun. But at least it's something to aim for and we should keep a mental eye open as to why we let certain people annoy us.

Hurting other people hurts you more

When you deliberately hurt someone mentally or physically you cause them pain and maybe you'll feel better for a while. In the long run, however, you'll feel worse. That's because doing something negative is never going to have positive results. I'm not suggesting you let people walk all over you but doing anything that has the sole intention of hurting someone else is likely to hurt you more.

Take time to say 'thank you'

In his masterwork *Civilisation*, Kenneth Clarke concluded that the hallmark of great civilization was institutionalized courtesy. By courtesy he meant having regard for the feelings of others. Saying 'thank you' and 'please' are the essential lubricants of courteous behavior and are worth more than money.

If it feels wrong, it is wrong

Wherever it comes from, we all have a conscience. We all instinctively know whether something is right or wrong. If you are about to do something and you think that it might be wrong, then pause. An inner voice will always tell you what is right and what is wrong. And if you don't listen to this voice before you act, you'll certainly hear it after you've acted.

Love, support and protect your family

The biggest investment in your life is that which your parents put into bringing you up and that which you will put into your children to bring them up. The return on this investment is happiness, stability, love, support, friendship and all the other good things in life.

Don't wait to be asked

People who need help often don't realize it. Help when and where you see help is needed without waiting to be asked. All progress in life is made by those who volunteer to make it. If you spend your life waiting to be asked you might run out of time and have made no difference to anyone.

Give as much as you take

There is more pleasure in life giving than taking. Of course, you have to have something to give before you can share it. But the rule is, the more you have, the more you should give. Wealth, health, happiness and luck are not distributed evenly in the world. If you have more than your fair share of any of them, make sure you spread a little of your good fortune (and don't wait to be asked).

Keep your desk and conscience clear

Do your job honestly and to the best of your ability. Behave honestly and according to your conscience. Go to bed knowing that you have done your best in both and you will sleep soundly. (Unless you live next door to a nightclub specializing in the loudest music on earth.)

A belief system provides a built-in check system: Is this consistent with what I believe in? Is it good? Does it add to the sum of human happiness?

It's your personal vision and values and, like corporate vision and values, only has any worth if it affects behavior.

being

innervation

momentum

How to be good

◆ Listen

◆ Be generous with your talents

◆ Don't speak ill of the living

◆ Hurting other people hurts you more

◆ Take time to say 'thank you'

◆ If it feels wrong, it is wrong

◆ Love, support and protect your family

◆ Don't wait to be asked

◆ Give as much as you take

◆ Keep your desk and conscience clear

How to be good in a bad world

The thing to bear in mind about any list of how to be good is that there should be a companion list of the 100 reasons why it's not a perfect world and why things go badly wrong. It's not an ideal world, there are a lot of bad things in it, and nothing is simple. So you need to crash test your new ten commandments and your instructions for being good.

Lessons learned the hard way

Ask yourself, on a scale of one to ten, how grown up you think you are. Chances are you're a generous marker and you've probably given yourself eight or nine. Anything under five and this book is way above your reading level. Most of us think we are pretty grown up, but what exactly is the process of growing up and maturing? You recognize it when you see it or achieve it but it's difficult to put your finger on what exactly is happening.

What has happened is that you've learned lessons, many of them the hard way. By going through a series of experiences, some of them painful, you know a lot now that you didn't know then.

As a general rule, the more painful the experience, the better you learn the lesson.

That's why most job advertisements specify at least two years' experience. This is a crafty way of saying that they want somebody else to have paid for the first two years of monstrous business cock ups and painful learning experiences.

Apart from those people who were wrapped in thick cotton wool by their mothers, most of us go through a series of challenges, experiences and learning processes. The key distinction is what you do with all those learning experiences. If you have the experiences and don't learn from them, then you are fated to keep repeating the same experiences again and again until you either learn the lesson or die.

Often, in a brainstorm about people issues, I ask people to write down lessons that they've learned the hard way. When the people in the group feed back their lessons, there is usually a very reverent atmosphere in the group as if people were telling stories of great personal heroism at the battlefront. In a way it's true because the lessons they've learned all have accompanying pain.

Over the last year or so I've compiled a list of the top lessons learned the hard way. This list is useful for several reasons. First, it shows you where the painful lessons usually are and, surprise, surprise, they come from dealing with other people – the danger of having

- Never hit a jellyfish with a spade
- Never work with friends
- The harder the decision, the better the outcome
- Not everyone likes you all of the time
- Losing control means losing the argument
- Never assume
- Confront bullies
- Trust your instincts
- Everything takes longer
- Don't trust 'authority'
- Don't play with matches

- No effort, no reward
- Details matter
- Make sure instructions are understood
- Be nice on the way up
- You can't do everything by yourself
- Get it in writing
- Understand the value of 'no'
- Understand others' aspirations
- Other people have other standards
- Get it in writing
- You have the right to get what you want
- Don't assume support in a crisis

assumptions and expectations of other people's behavior, and the difficulty of communicating with them and establishing efficient and friendly working relationships.

The second lesson (and I'm sorry about all the lessons in this chapter) is that the list comprises a hugely valuable storehouse of wisdom. Again the difficulty is remembering and applying all the lessons. They all make sense when you read them on a piece of paper, but until you've lived through them and internalized them, it's difficult to behave immediately in accordance with them. However, when you've given yourself time to think, it's a very useful exercise to remind yourself of what lessons you have learned and the pain which goes with them if you don't follow them.

When, occasionally, it's possible to get some sort of perspective on your life and the lessons you've learned in it, there generally

- Value your own judgement
- Don't neglect yourself
- Be careful who you trust
- Don't be too open too soon
- Beware of those you threaten
- Constantly communicate upwards
- Keep things in perspective
- Comply when necessary
- Stick to strategy
- Stick to the facts
- Deal with things quickly
- Don't let things fester

- Involve people in decisions
- Occasionally be ruthless
- Think how others will react
- Clarify tasks
- Keep your mouth shut
- Keep things simple
- Get the right information
- Don't trust everyone
- Never pretend to know what you don't
- Don't talk of wings – try to fly

being

seems to be a pattern that things in life are sent to you in order for you to learn from them. That's why people often say, 'I'm very glad I went through that because it's got me where I am today which is a much better place.'

Remember, you are a one-person learning organization.

innervation

If you can approach everything in life as an opportunity to widen and deepen your experience and as a valuable lesson to be learned, you actually reduce the pain you suffer. That's because the experience itself becomes less of an emotional odyssey, and more of an objective learning experience. (Please don't quote that back to me when I'm having my next big learning experience.)

momentum

Finally, it's worth remembering that other people, generally but not always younger than you, have yet to learn some of these lessons. It is a key part of management to help people through the pitfalls that you've already identified because it won't help you watching them go through an unnecessarily painful learning experience. On the other hand, sometimes you just have to let people get on with it and find out the hard way. If you're not actively engaged in the process, this can actually be a very rewarding spectator sport.

Warning: If you're concerned about political correctness skip the next chapter (and all the others because you've clearly got used to having other people make up your mind for you). How can anything be political and correct at the same time?

being

innervation

momentum

sexual politics – who's on top?

True equality exists in the treatment of unequal things unequally.

Aristotle

One of the clearest and most profound changes in working practices in the late twentieth century has been the full participation of women in the workplace. There are few places left where women don't work alongside men on an equal footing and most of those places women wouldn't choose to go anyway.

Naturally, there are still inequalities here and there and women in Britain are still penalized in the working world for having children. However, things continue to change in the right direction for women who want to work. The new economy with its more flexible approach to work will accelerate this trend.

Allied to this is the fact that the new economy is moving away from making and selling towards relationships and service. At the same time, management is moving from command and control to support and communicate. All these are considered to be more feminine traits, which is why people talk about an increasingly feminized workplace.

Many books have been written about how men and women are from different planets in their personal and emotional lives. But political correctness dictates that men and women have to be treated equally at work. This is a mistake. Equal opportunity, yes, equal treatment, no.

It goes back to the new commandments: treat people how they would like to be treated. Men and women work differently, they think differently and they should be treated differently.

The new economy is about individuals and a thumping great difference between individuals is whether they are male or female.

For women only

Understanding male behavior at work

These days everyone who walks erect in business accepts that there is no real difference between the sexes and that they're both absolutely equal in terms of talent, professionalism and ambition.

In fact this is a myth put about by women to make men feel better about themselves, because in most areas of business, apart from lifting heavy engine blocks, women have men well and truly whipped.

Many women find male behavior at work baffling at best and astonishingly brutish at worst. The answer to all this is in evolution and the fact that mentally men are all still best adapted to prehistory when a man's place was behind a mammoth. Many men at work still feel that their place is behind a mammoth with all the occupational hazards that entails. But, in reality, the modern workplace is a female place where consensus, communication and organizational skills are at a premium.

In prehistory, men didn't really need to hunt as the women grew 80 per cent of the food. Instead, men hunted to prove just how macho they were. Let's face it, if food were the issue, men would be out there hunting sheep, but how impressive would that have looked in cave paintings. In business, the activity closest to hunting is sales and that's why there is a preponderance of men in it. They get into their cars and go out hunting for the big sales which they then report

being

innervation

momentum

back in triumph, generally with highly inflated figures and before the ink is on the contract. National Account Managers are the biggest, hairiest hunters of them all, bringing back sales so colossal that the company nearly collapses under the strain of having to digest them.

Evolution isn't about survival of the fittest, it's about survival of those who can reproduce best. That is why virtually everything men do at work is some sort of sexual display.

This ranges from the big Porsche-driving displays to the smaller, everyday pen twiddling and trouser fiddling. Shouting in meetings is exactly what stags do during the mating season and crushing other weaker males is precisely what bull walruses do on the beach.

Or another example: only men put their feet up on the desk. Nobody puts their feet up on the desk because it's comfortable. In reality, it's a male display thing – I can loll around like the lion king because when I choose to kill it's feast time for the whole jungle. Men have other bodily habits which involve the noisy expulsion of air at high pressure from both ends. Again both these habits are sexual displays in that they are supposed to communicate, 'Yes, I am a big hunter, and I have feasted well on meat. Breed with me.' Strangely, this and all the other male displays have the exact opposite effect on women who, in any case, are all far too busy doing 80 per cent of the useful work.

Men had only just started to walk upright when they walked into the office. Which is why you see so much buttock baring, chest beating and gonad scratching. Male chest beating comes in the form of talking at huge length in meetings and then complaining when the meetings over-run. Buttock baring is now restricted to manly phrases such as 'going balls out on a project', or it being 'cock on block time'. Strangely, when things go wrong, you won't find men rushing to get the block out.

Men are happy if they have two things: confidence in their performance and a good selection of toys. Men like toys because they know they can perform with them. Hence the popularity of high-performance cars with low-performance men. Men who can't perform or lose their toys tend to shout. The more they're upset, the more they shout. If shouting fails, men try the subtle approach of having a quiet drink at the pub. Sadly, alcohol tends to make men shout louder and shout complete rubbish. The best way to take the sting out of a raging ego at full blast is to say, 'Sounds like you're angry about that, Brian.' This acknowledges that you've heard the big jungle sound of him beating his chest and then you can get to the root of the big strategic issue that's upset him, like not remembering his birthday or whatever.

Modern women run businesses, raise families, support the arts and have regular thundering orgasms – women call this juggling their lives. When men say they are juggling their lives you can take this to mean a state of continuous balls up.

The only balls men keep in continuous motion are the ones in their pockets.

Juggling is a bit of a circus act and men can't stand the fact that they can't do it as well as women. That's why when women are busy juggling, men try to grab attention with other circus acts such as lion taming, fire eating, sword swallowing and getting shot from the end of a cannon – all in a day's work for your typical male sales executive.

All in all, this notion of a feminized workplace is probably just another male conspiracy to create a crèche culture in the workplace to reduce competition at the sharp end. Supportive mentoring, empathy and coaching is supposed to be the feminized management style of the future. But let's face it, too much coaching, empathy and supportive listening and you won't be able to say the things vital for managing stroppy, aggressive men who think coaching is for Saga holidays, i.e., 'shut up', 'you're wrong', 'I don't care', and 'we're doing it my way'.

Never forget that all men have the sexual sophistication of a small dog. However successful a woman you are and whatever you're doing in business, the men you manage will be thinking about sex every nine seconds, quite possibly with you. Which means you have about eight seconds to get your message over.

Being a working woman – what's it all about?

Creativity

Women's brains are wired differently than men's. They tend to think more holistically about a problem. They tend to see the bigger picture and the complexities of relationships more clearly. They tend to make longer-lasting decisions.

Consistency

Men's behavior is affected by their testosterone. They have very primitive sexual drive that gets translated into aggression at work which in turn is translated into dangerous and ill-thought-through decisions. Women make a decision on its merits, not on how good it will make them look to the opposite sex.

Kindness

More business decisions need to take into account the needs and feelings of staff and customers. Women naturally do this better.

Communication

Men communicate only when they have to, which is often far too late. Women are naturally communicative and better at sharing information.

Being a mom

There won't be any more working women if working women don't have babies. It's a tough double act but women are a lot better equipped to do it than men.

Being a breadwinner

It's a sad fact that more and more men are finding it difficult to get a job. It's more than likely that women will be the major earners in a family and will continue to be even while they're bringing up children.

For men only

How women behave at work

The future is a woman – if she doesn't change her mind. They say that the future is a woman because in life, business and community, relationships between individuals will become increasingly important. Women forget that most relationships also have a man involved. Men just don't feel the need to talk about it all the time.

Of course women have many inbuilt advantages in business. Any woman who can run a house full of screaming children will have no trouble participating in board-level discussions; any woman who has ever warmed a bottle with one hand and changed a diaper with the other will have no difficulty working with an advertising agency; and any woman who has been in continuous labor for eight hours will have no trouble sitting through a presentation from the head of IT.

Female bonding

Men who work with women on a regular basis know that they are like visitors from another company in Eastern Europe: a lot of what they do is familiar but they do it in ways that are often puzzling. For example, women in the office bond in different ways to men, often swapping notes on dress, hair and general appearance. This is a very fine skill that takes a lifetime to acquire and men should not wade in with, 'You look fat in that old dress and the haircut doesn't help.'

Men and women have very different ways of bonding in the office.

Gratuitous compliments about hair and clothing are the entry level stuff for women.

'That's a nice blouse', is the female equivalent of 'Did you see the football game?' The next level for a man would be, 'What team do you support?' For women the next stage is swapping all the innermost secrets of every relationship they've ever had.

The feminized workplace

It's pretty much accepted by everybody that the workplace is becoming increasingly feminized and that the skills you need to have in business are the more feminine skills of listening, caring, compassion, empathy and great all-round communication. This will come as a bitter blow to all those women who have been carving their way to the top of organizations through sheer ability, determination and raw ambition.

Women take things personally which can be great because they take a human perspective and don't get over-analytical. On the other hand, you have to be careful when you say something like, '*the company needs downsizing,*' in case they take it personally and spend all evening on the scales.

Women are exceptionally good at listening rather than talking (as they never tire of telling anyone who will listen). A woman listening sympathetically is at her most dangerous because in the space of a cup of tea and a biscuit you can reveal your secret hopes and deepest fears and then, later on, a succession of other women will listen to the first woman passing on your secret hopes and deepest fears.

Women also like to think that they are better at multi-tasking and juggling their lives. This is why women can't throw, because they're so busy juggling. In the game of life do you want someone who can throw and pass the ball, or someone who can juggle it?

Powerful, intelligent and high-earning women

There are a lot of powerful, intelligent and high-earning women around in business and there's likely to be a lot more around in the future. It's going to be a fact of life. Like other facts of life it's best to know about them, accept them and not get embarrassed about them.

Some men find it very difficult to work for a woman or, even more dangerously, find it difficult to accept that their partner earns more money than them. There are two approaches to this:

◆ If you're really worried about your masculinity you can pump iron, take up boxing lessons and join the foreign legion.

◆ Or you can get your attitude into the 21st century.

If you're going to be undermined by people who are cleverer or more successful than you are, whatever sex they are, then you're going to spend most of your life undermined. Earn some self-respect and then respect the achievements of others. Either you love your partner or you don't. And if she's got the brains and grit to be holding down a good job then she's probably worth hanging onto.

Being a modern man – what's it all about?

In business there are some things where having balls and a full measure of testosterone are still useful.

Creativity

Men's brains are wired differently to women's. They tend to think along more linear lines; they're more penetrative; they tend to get to the heart of an argument faster; they're better at quick decision making and creative thinking.

Consistency

Women's behavior is affected by their hormones. It happens at home and it also happens at work. Sometimes it means they can get things out of proportion. Sometimes they cry. This doesn't mean a business catastrophe, it just means they're having a 'bad hair' day.

Aggression

Sometimes you need to act quickly, decisively and boldly. Men are good at this. Businesses may be becoming more feminized but they still compete against each other and competition is a male thing.

Communication

Women communicate whether they need to or not. This wastes a lot of time and clogs up the channels when rapid, one-way communication is needed.

being

innervation

momentum

Being a dad

Kids need dads. Otherwise the next generation of little boys are going to have an even harder time of it in the workplace.

Being a breadwinner

Women, unlike men, often have a choice in their lives. They can work or they can bring up a family or do both. If they choose to stay at home and bring up the family, then it's your responsibility to be the breadwinner. (And of course be supportive at home at the same time.)

Working couples

When you're young free and single, it doesn't matter how bad a day you have at work because in the evening you can go out and drink until you forget your work, your boss and where you live. When you're older, this is replaced by going home and having a high-octane whine to your partner.

People up and down the country must think that where their partners work is an absolute technical and administrative shambles, run by cretinous bullying managers with half-baked, unworkable ideas, lackadaisically implemented by offices full of petty, egotistical shirkers. And if it weren't for their partner, no useful work would get done at all.

At home, the accepted way to respond to these work whines is just to say at regular intervals, 'That's terrible, would you like a cup of tea.' What you should absolutely not say is, 'Well, if you're not happy there, get another job.' Advice from partners ranges from the unhelpful to the downright dangerous. The most common advice is, 'Well, you should just tell him where to stick it!' This is, of course, the one thing your partner can't do, which is why they're moaning in the first place.

When both partners work, there are other rules to be observed. For example, when your loved one comes home from work and says, 'Our new IT system is worse than the old one,' the natural reaction is to say, 'You're lucky you've got one that works. We've been continually upgrading for the last six years, without anything ever working.' The urge to horror-trump should always be resisted. If in doubt, make tea.

Remember, however bad your day at work has been, your partner's day will always have been much worse. If you're going to make a serious claim for having had the worst day you must make sure you get home last, as your claim simply won't carry any weight if you're home first, in front of the TV with your slippers on.

Over the course of an average year's whining, you absorb an enormous amount of detailed and delicate information about your partner's company. The time to make use of all this is at the Christmas party where you can casually feed back all sorts of highly speculative gossip. This makes up for the pain of being invited in the first place.

After all, this is the same company that has made your partner miserable for the last 12 months and now expects you to have dinner with your partner's boss so she can demonstrate all those personality traits that make her so loathsome to work for. If companies really wanted to show partners a good time, they would give them a Christmas bonus for all the counselling and therapy they've done throughout the year.

thinking

don't leave creativity to accountants

There's nothing new under the sun, but there's always a better way.

Ed McCabe, Scottish eccentric and future Jack Welch

Anyone over 30 reading this book may remember a time when the most important thing on the corporate agenda was quality. TQM was the big, buzzy acronym and it stood for Total Quality Management. What that actually meant was something as simple as getting things right; making things that didn't fall apart; delivering them on time; and having a workforce that actually got on together.

Anyone under 30 will think that was a pretty bizarre thing to get excited about in management terms but anybody over 40 will tell them that quality and management and quality management used to be very, very thin on the ground.

Fortunately, we've made big strides in that direction and now that everyone realizes that quality is a pre-requisite for just about everything in business, the focus has shifted from how you do things to what things you do. This frees us all up to think about new and exciting things. Which means creativity and innovation.

Creativity is thinking new things, innovation is making them happen, and they are now both at the top of the corporate agenda. How can you tell? Because:

Creativity is what senior management require middle management to get from junior management.

Not sure who said this. Could be Jack Welch, CEO, General Electric

Creativity – why bother?

The best and most important reason is that fresh thinking keeps you ahead of the competition – because in the new economy it's not the big that eat the small, it's the quick that eat the slow. The quickest-witted, quickest-acting companies will eat the lunch of slow, dim-witted companies.

There's nothing new about innovation. We've all been doing it since the stone ages which is the main reason we're no longer in the stone ages. What has changed is the pace of innovation. In the Stone Ages we invented fire and then sat around for 10,000 years hoping someone would invent the marshmallow. Now we can't wait more than a few months for the latest trousers, music, 2-in-1 shampoo and conditioner or military hardware.

Fashion is everything. Consumers are only interested in what is the latest and best and if you can't think of it someone else will.

Companies and businesses need to be at the cutting edge.

They want to employ people who have the skills, instinct and courage to work at the cutting edge and the tenacity to keep moving that edge forward.

More than any other, the people who will be valued in the new economy are those who can think for themselves and think creatively about the areas they are in. And the reason for that is because in the new economy, software equals hard cash.

thinking

innovation

momentum

Software = hard cash

In the new economy business fortunes are now made in services and software. The wider definition of software includes anything created in your brain and imagination – like music, computer programs, a Hollywood screenplay, a new prescription drug or a new way of packaging financial services.

Pokémon was and is a massive money-maker. It is sophisticated software from the imaginations of its creators backed up by very sophisticated marketing. The Pokémon phenomenon at its height was making more money per day than the entire economy of Cambodia. (I actually made that up. That's rule 4a. Creativity helps you tell massive porkies.)

Viagra is another piece of software (stop it). A piece of pure research and imagination and a product that has produced explosive growth (stop it) for its parent company Pfizer. Think of the profits waiting for the first company to produce a legal, non-addictive, mind-altering drug.

Brief digression

Some experts say that the global drug trade now is the equivalent of a G7 economy. What's interesting about the drug trade is how creative it is in its whole production and distribution process. For example, in Colombia they found a submarine being constructed in the mountains which was intended to be taken to the Pacific and then used to ferry cargoes under the world's oceans and under the noses of the world's policemen. If it weren't illegal and downright unhealthy, the drug trade would make a fascinating example of how a well-financed, customer-driven innovation process can work.

Business is where creativity is at

If you're interested in using your imagination to benefit mankind and also to make a living, business is now the place to do it.

There is more creative thinking happening in the business world than there is in the arts. Art has lost its function of interpreting the world and now is looking for a role beyond that of being just another commodity for speculators.

The biggest thing we've had in the arts world in the last decade is a sliced sheep in a perspex case. In business, we've had those for years. They're called sandwiches. There's more artistry in a Dyson vacuum cleaner than there is in the entire Turner Prize.

Being good in business is the most fascinating kind of art.

Not Jack Welch but the artist Andy Warhol, who knew what he was talking about because he was a very successful businessman. (You can make your own mind up about the art.)

Politics, especially in the Victorian era, was full of energy and enthusiasm for improving people's lot. Now the tolerance of the electorate for creative political thinking, from either the left or right, is extremely narrow and it is matched by a distinct lack of vision and political courage by all the major parties.

Science is more creative than art and politics. Why? Because science is the last area of thought that isn't hamstrung by post-modern introspection.

(That's what my postman says and I'm not going to argue.) But business is what plugs arts and science into real life. It's exciting, sexy and absolutely vital.

People's lives are affected more by business and technological innovation than by politics. And by that I mean the Internet, mobile phones, microwaved meals, television, etc. In the last 20 years there has been more creative thinking in managing airports than in managing the economy.

Excuses not to be creative

Sadly, many people in business have mentally outsourced creative thinking. Many people in business instinctively say, 'I'm not creative.' Think of the job you're currently doing. Now think of the CV you wrote to get that job. According to that you're a multi-lingual, team-playing perfectionist. Now that's what I call creative writing.

Often people think they're not creative because they believe creativity lies somewhere else and is the responsibility of other people who live on the cutting edge of fashion. Not so.

Let me talk about people who are paid to be creative, i.e., designers and advertising creatives. There are a few geniuses, people who in other centuries would have been court painters or poets. They have natural talent and where it comes from is a bit of a mystery.

I am merely a conduit for the untrammelled superabundance of God.

That's what Felix Mendelssohn said about how he composed music. He just sat down and inspiration flowed through him. Darwin said that the Theory of Evolution came to him complete in a flash of inspiration and the rest of his life was spent backing it up with scientific observation.

However, the other 90 per cent of creative people are no more creative than anybody else in their office or many other offices. What they do have is the training, experience and most importantly the environment to be creative.

For example, let's say I wanted you to think creatively about a new kind of yogurt and I gave you a day off to think about it. Even before you started thinking, you would have a 100 per cent better chance of being creative because of the three things I have just given you:

QUIET

TIME

PERMISSION

These are the three things you normally won't have. 'Creative' people in agencies have all three in abundance.

So let's accept for a moment that most people are capable of being creative in the right circumstances. What are the right circumstances? Some say that they need to be alone to think, others that they need to chew the fat, brainstorm, etc. What both these approaches have in common is that they involve making new connections; the former in the individual's mind, the latter between two or more people.

It's too risky

Everyone knows that if you do what you always do, you get what you always get. This is actually a great source of comfort to most people.

The familiar is good, habit is good, the known is good.

Everything else is dark, unknown and scary. Worse than anything else, doing things differently is a risk. And we all know what happens in business when you take a risk.

What happens when you take a risk

You take a risk, you lose your job, you start to drink, your marriage goes, then it's drug addiction, prostitution, impotence, madness, death. We've all been there.

In business the only risk is to take no risks at all. It's not enough to be in the right place now because you will be overtaken by other individuals and organizations who are prepared to take risks and explore the unknown.

We can't think outside the box because someone's sitting on the lid

The cliché for creative thinking in business is thinking outside the box. It comes from this little puzzle. How do you join all the dots using four linked straight lines?

•　　•　　•

•　　•　　•

•　　•　　•

The secret is to go outside the box. For some reason people who don't know the answer stay rigidly inside the box.

As a metaphor it's actually quite useful because in business we are usually thinking within a whole sequence of boxes. It's vital to be aware of these constraints on your thinking before you even attempt to think creatively.

Box 1: your job description

You're a banker so you think like a banker. You're in IT so you think like an IT person. You're a dentist so every problem is oral. You're a psychologist so every problem needs therapy, etc. How much is your profession causing you to think in well-worn professional grooves?

Notice how when the Millennium Dome was in trouble they hired someone from Disney because they wanted someone who thought about things in a theme park kind of way. Then when the Dome got in real trouble they brought in an accountant because they wanted someone to think about things in a profit and loss kind of way.

Box 2: your box in the organogram

Pretty much all businesses have a little organogram that shows who does what. They're just a collection of boxes based on job descriptions but those little boxes and lines condition how you think and who you talk to. Far better to think of everyone being in a big melting pot and feeling free to talk to whoever they feel like talking to.

Box 3: your key performance indicators

All jobs are measured. Generally you are given six or eight performance indicators or key tasks or measurements.

In business, as in life, you get what you measure.

This is another major constraint on creative thinking.

Imagine your job was to reduce congestion at Heathrow. What six things would you measure? There are so many things you can measure that each group of six amounts to a separate job description.

Job description 1	Job description 2	Job description 3
Length of lines at check-in	Number of flights	Toilet cubicles in use
Length of taxi rank	Size of planes	Security breaches
Time taken to get to airport	Delays to flights	Morale of staff
Time taken to get through airport	Landing intervals	Shop profitability
Wait at baggage carousel	Number of runways	Carpet wear
Number of passengers	Crashes	VIP suite usage

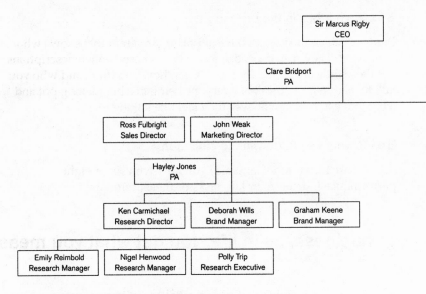

Here's your box – make sure you stay in it

Sticking to what you measure means you'll never escape from old thinking. For example, if you were job description 1, you could solve all your problems by having one additional measurement if that measurement was how many airports there are in the UK. Build another one and you'll halve all your other measurements at a stroke.

Box 4: the business box

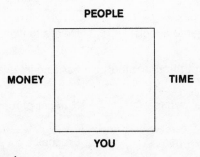

The business strong box

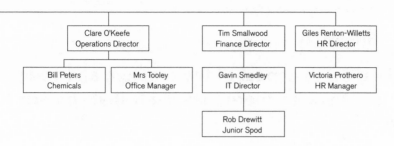

Everybody in business works within constraints of time, people and money. Few people have enough of any of them and their thinking about the business is constrained by the thought that they don't have enough time, people or money to do things differently.

If any of you have been in a company that has gone through severe downsizing you will know that, after the tears have been shed, there is a tremendous amount of creativity unleashed as workers have to find new ways of doing things with dramatically reduced resources.

At the other end of the scale, huge advances can be made when money is thrown at a project. The reason the Americans put a man on the moon is because they spent 4 per cent of their GDP over a decade doing so.

You can release creative thinking without any real change in your existing resources. You simply have to imagine how you would do things with half or double the people, time or money. For example, if I asked you to think about how you would improve road repairs with double the people, time and money you might come up with the ideas of specialist planners and repairers, 24-hour working, and better-paid workers.

The ideas here are sound. The trick is to make them work with your existing resources. So instead of separate specialists you could train your existing staff better so that they were multi-skilled. If you can't work for 24 hours perhaps you could just work at night when there's less traffic. And if you can't afford a blanket pay rise then introduce performance-related pay.

The fourth side of the box is you.

If you've solved every aspect of the problem and you still have a problem, then it's more than likely that you are the problem.

This whole book is about how to make sure you're not the problem in any business environment you inhabit.

Let's have a look at the way you think and see if that's holding you back.

Creativity – it's not what you think

Actually thinking about the problem is 90 per cent of the way to coming up with a solution. But thinking is such a scary thing to do that most people instinctively try to avoid it. Creative thinking is where you're not satisfied with the first thought that pops into your head and instead you see whether there might not be a better thought or simply a different thought.

Many creative gurus with impressive daily rates will tell you how important it is to be like a child when it comes to creative thinking. It's true that children have fewer assumptions, knowledge and experience than adults and therefore are not constrained by them. However, children don't really do creative thinking, not the sort that is useful in business at any rate.

It's actually highly dangerous to encourage business people, especially from the marketing department, to release their inner child. What would be far more impressive is if they could release their inner adult with the full power and potential of the adult mind. The first step to doing this, as in so much in life, is to know yourself.

In everyone's life there is a mental puberty every bit as powerful as physical puberty.

Often this mental puberty is completely ignored in the massive hormonal maelstrom of the teenage years. Sometime in your teens, you suddenly become aware that you are either left or right wing, naturally optimistic or pessimistic, a creative or logical individual, someone who is tough or tender minded. These, for whatever reasons, are your natural inclinations and they will colour your thinking for as long as you are unaware of them.

We're all completely different so it should come as no surprise that we all think in a different way. Just to give you an example of how deeply etched your thinking patterns already are, try answering the following questions:

◆ How confident or shy are you?

◆ How right or left wing are you?

◆ How optimistic or pessimistic are you?

◆ How aggressive or passive are you?

◆ How masculine or feminine are you?

◆ How visual or numerical are you?

◆ How logical or emotional are you?

There are no right or wrong answers in this quiz. But you can imagine that a pessimistic left-winger who thought very logically and had yet to explore his feminine side would think in a very different way to somebody who was a right-wing optimist who tended to think creatively in a more feminine way. It doesn't matter where you come on this spectrum, but it does matter that you are aware of where you are and how this affects the way you think.

Rule number one for creativity is to think.

That's the hard part. But then the advanced lesson is to think about the way you think and to see how that restricts and fashions your options. The definition of being narrow minded is to believe that the way you think is the only way to think.

Once you understand your default thinking mode you can turn it off and let your mind range all around any problem and attack it from any direction. It's liberating personally and professionally.

Your universe

The illustration below is a visual representation of your thoughts compared to all the other thoughts you could possibly have. The thought in the middle represents the tip of an iceberg, the iceberg being all the old well-trodden routes through your brain. This slice of pizza represents the way you have accumulated and arranged your mental furniture. Mentally it's where you're at home. Mentally, most people like to stay at home because venturing out of the mental comfort zone is a DIY nightmare for the mind which can often be an uncomfortable and eye-opening experience.

Thoughts don't arrive from nowhere. They're like job applicants: they've got a lot of education behind them, they seem very plausible but they often don't stand up to rigorous examination.

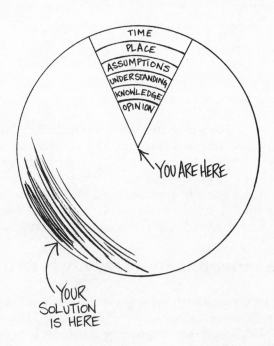

The universe

Behind every thought is an opinion: if you don't support foxhunting you're unlikely to have a positive thought about it. Behind your opinions is your knowledge of the subject. After all, you usually form your opinions on the basis of the facts you have at your disposal. Facts, of course, are only a slim part of the truth and the facts you have in your head will be only a partial understanding of the entire problem. When presented with a different set of facts people will sometimes change their opinion. But not often. That's because what's behind knowledge and facts is more important mentally – by that we mean our deeper understanding and assumptions.

Assumptions are fossilized opinions that you don't need to bother thinking about any more.

Similarly, behind your understanding there is a full range of assumptions that you will be making often unconsciously.

You can imagine just how dangerous and obstructive assumptions are when it comes to accessing fresh thinking. And, finally, your assumptions are generally the product of the place you are in and the time you are in. By time and place we mean both the large-scale and the small-scale. Where you were born and raised and the culture you're part of are obviously very important to the way you think. Clearly, the age in which you live is also a big factor in your mental processes: compare the child of the Sixties to a child of the Eighties.

On a much smaller scale, time and place are equally important. How you think when you're sitting at the boardroom table is a lot different to when you're 500 yards away on the shop floor. Similarly, how you think during the recession is different from the way you think during the boom times.

If you are to keep your mind alert to the millions of other possibilities in any given situation, it's absolutely vital that you have a clear understanding of your own mental iceberg and that you have analyzed how your thinking is continually affected by time and place, and how your knowledge and understanding and assumptions are all intimately related, and are specific to you.

Once you know where you're starting from, it's much easier to get somewhere else and it is the mark of all great thinkers that their

thinking

innervation

momentum

starting point has been to know themselves. Descartes famously said, 'I think, therefore I am.' The second step on from this is you are what you think. And we all know how it works. If you think you're super-confident you generally are super-confident. If you think you're a worthless piece of dirt, then that's what you'll be before long. Therefore, if you want to change who you are, the best place to start is with the way you think.

You can do this in two ways.

- ◆ The first way is to use your personal opinions, knowledge, understanding and experience in a more effective manner.
- ◆ The second way is to look for new opinions, knowledge, understanding and experience other than those you currently have.

Let's prove just how non-linear and creative we are and start with the second way.

creativity part 2 – there's nothing for you here

Pet food is a huge industry. It's not a very complex industry because cats and dogs aren't quite as choosy as we are in their consumption habits. In fact, most of their choices in this sector are made by human beings for very human reasons. I'm sure I'm not allowed to say this, but most cats and dogs would be equally healthy and happy on the cheapest, own-brand food in the supermarket. In fact pets have been around a lot longer than pet food. But how good would we feel about our role as carer/provider for our little fluffkins if we offered them any old pet food or even the scraps from the kitchen.

It's a very competitive market, pet food, and the big manufacturers are continually innovating around the subject. Imagine for a moment you worked for one of these companies and you had been tasked to come up with some fantastic new ideas for cat food. Because you're a well-educated, intelligent and, dare I say, good-looking individual, you would probably have no problem coming up with a great range of ideas. For the first few minutes, that is, and then thinking of anything exciting or new would become increasingly difficult.

At this juncture we would call for the help of one of the most creative individuals ever to have existed: Albert Einstein. Between discovering things about the universe that God thought he had kept a closely guarded secret, Einstein said the following:

You can't solve a problem with the same thinking that created it.

In a nutshell, this describes the difficulty of escaping from all the thoughts, opinions, assumptions and experiences that wedge you firmly into the tight mental spot that gives you your problem.

Start thinking somewhere else

In order to start accessing fresh thinking about cat food you need to start your thinking somewhere else. It doesn't matter where, but preferably it will be as far away from cats and cat food as possible so as to avoid any duplication of knowledge, opinions, understanding and experience.

Take for example the glass of water sitting on the desk in front of me. Just a glass of water, nothing interesting about that. But there was probably nothing interesting about cat food until you gave it your undivided attention. Once you start examining and thinking about the glass of water it actually has all sorts of interesting values, appearances, features and properties. For example it's a container, it's a liquid, there's surface tension on the water, it's full of little bubbles, the glass is transparent, it has a thick base.

Now apply that thinking to cat food and all sorts of fascinating possibilities suggest themselves.

Container

Start thinking around the subject of a container and you start to question why cat food comes in a tin. Not a friendly thing to use, not easy to store, not easy to open. Why not have the cat food in a series of frozen briquettes which can be microwaved to room temperature and then eaten. Or why not sell the cat food in the dish from which the cat eats it. Or have a little travel dish full of food.

Surface tension

You could have thought about cat food until you were blue in the face and you still wouldn't have considered the concept of surface tension. But now you've got this fantastic new concept to play with in your thinking about cat food. For example, why not have a tin of cat food that can be opened by the cat itself so that it can feed itself while you're away. If they can get through cat flaps, they can certainly open a tin of cat food.

Bubbles

Edible balls of cat food. The cat plays with its food until bored and then eats it. Or perhaps there are tiny little croutons in the cat food to keep cats' teeth sharp.

Transparent

Try clear packaging of cat food, especially if the food is worth looking at. Or sell the cat food on the transparency of the production and supply process so that you are famous for the quality and ethical virtue of your food.

Thick base

A layered cat food. A meaty bottom layer overlaid with a bed of rice and topped off with a cheesy gratin finish.

Liquid

Cat soup. (This is soup for your cat not soup made from your cat although I admire the way your mind was working there.)

All these ideas for improving cat food came because we stopped thinking about cat food and started thinking about something entirely different. All we have to do now is make sure the ideas are patented up to the gills, sit back and wait for the huge cash offers to pour in from the pet food companies.

Of course it doesn't have to be cat food and you don't have to think about a glass of water. You can have any problems in the world and you can use anything else in the world to give you the mental ammunition to take on and subdue the problem.

It is perfectly possible to make creative connections between any two things in the universe. Let me show you how it is done with another example.

Your desk calculator as stimulus for innovating in yogurt

Aspect of calculator	Thought stimulated	Idea for yogurt
Plastic	Credit card	Calorie barcode swiper
Buttons	Chocolate buttons	Mini-chocolate buttons in yogurt
Solar powered	Heat from sun	Self-warming lunch yogurt
Raised head	Baby bottle teat	Slurper top for eating on the move
Screen	Mini plasma screen	On-pack text messaging advertising
SHARP	Bitter	Alcoholic yogurt for lunchtime drinking
Memory	Childhood	Retro anniversary packaging
Rectangular	Lego	Pots that click together for kids' games
Rubber feet	Frogs	Luminescent green, slime horror yogurt
Off button	Going off	Lid changes color when going off
Numbers	Lottery	Lotto yogurt
Square root	Ginseng root	Health yogurt for me
Made in China	CAN'T THINK OF ONE	NO IDEA

thinking

innervation

momentum

Amazing results

By looking at these simple objects close to hand we now have several potentially marketable ideas for yogurt. I'm not suggesting that we've achieved a major breakthrough but the above list could be put together in about five minutes of thinking. A marketing consultancy would charge you many thousands of pounds to get not much better results at the end of a fearsomely expensive brainstorming day in the country. (See our website www.smokehouse.co.uk if you're interested.)

Think how many objects you could use in a day to give you new perspectives. You would get a very great many ideas that were absolute rubbish but in amongst the dross would almost certainly be gold. The trick is to keep trying.

The best way to have good ideas is to have lots of ideas.

Linus Pauling, Nobel Prize winning scientist, and possible acquaintance of Jack Welch

I'm too embarrassed to look at my calculator

The most difficult part of this whole process is deciding that you are going to stop thinking about the problem in the old way and start giving some serious attention to your calculator or any other object. Getting over this embarrassment factor seems to be the most difficult part of creative thinking for most people. But once you've got the hang of it, it really does come naturally and yields great results for the minimum of effort.

Before you know it, you'll find yourself on the train, working on a tricky accountancy problem by looking intently at the emergency handle.

Don't make it easy on yourself

Cynical people who are above this sort of thing often feel the need to point out that there is no creative thinking going on at all. What in fact you're doing is simply listing the properties of an object and then your brain goes back to thinking about the problem in question.

There is an element of truth in this, in so much that when one of the properties of your object immediately suggests something about your product, it may be that the connection is too close to be useful. In the example above, the calculator was plastic and my first thought was naturally that yogurt pots are also plastic. So my thoughts had gone straight back to my original problem.

There is a way around this problem and that is not to think about your problem again, but to think even harder about your stimulating object. For example, the next thing I thought about plastic was 'credit card' and this had all sorts of useful inspirational material for yogurt.

The rule here is when you are struggling for a new angle of inspiration, the key is to make the connection more remote and more difficult. Experience shows that the more you struggle to make the connection, the better the final idea will be. This makes sense really, as what you are in effect doing is thinking about your problem in a way that hasn't been done before. Using the properties of an object to stimulate new thinking is particularly useful when it comes to new product development.

When nothing comes to mind about a particular aspect, for example 'Made in China', you need to repeat the whole exercise of interrogation and expansion.

Made in China

Aspect of China	Thought stimulated	Idea for yogurt
Porcelain	Luxury	Luxury indulgent yogurt
Red	Indulgence and Catholicism	Contraceptive yogurt
Wall	Bricks	Lego yogurt
Cheap	Birds and bottle tops	Deliveries by milkman
Tiananmen Square	Democracy	Vote for new flavors
Junk	Junk food	Make packaging look like junk food
One child	Spoiled	Long-life yogurt

Just do it now

Have a go now. If you can't be bothered or are still flicking through to get hot tips on how to make more money, you better skip the rest of this chapter.

Starting your thinking somewhere else, making the connection back to your original subject, and applying the new perspective, is the absolute bedrock of creative thinking.

And don't forget the more difficult the connection the better the idea is likely to be. In brainstorming, when you tell somebody to tackle a problem like the Middle East crisis by examining how a shoe is put together there is often a laugh. This is a very clear indication that the person finds the connection preposterous. It's also a very clear indication that once they've got over their initial horror and embarrassment, the subject will generally prove rich in new perspectives and thinking on the problem. We call this the 'titter factor' and the bigger the titter, the bigger the idea.

Who are you looking at?

A very similar exercise can be done with people, famous people or people you know. With people, we are more interested in their particular approach to life in general and what their response would be to a particular problem. You can, of course, treat any person like an object and use his physical characteristics in the same way you would when describing a plum pudding. But for this example we'll concentrate on people's distinct approaches as this is more useful for tackling strategic and HR issues.

Let's take a random selection of people and see how they would tackle a very loose problem such as restructuring a department.

Person	Approach	Idea for restructuring department
Julie Andrews	Singing	Sing from same hymn sheet – common purpose
Ronald Reagan	Forgetfulness	Amnesty – fresh start – all old sins forgotten
Boadicea	Swords on chariot	Cut out dead wood
Lester Piggott	Speed	Act quickly
David Attenborough	Nature	Natural wastage or organic growth
My history teacher	Mad	Do the unexpected – make the big changes

The ideas aren't anything radical or new but what they do is to force you to think across a full range of options. Instead of a small tinkering with the department, thinking about Lester Piggott, Boadicea and my history teacher will have opened up the possibility that restructuring your department could be the chance to cut out all the dead wood and build something completely different that revolutionizes a way you do business. And of course to do this you need to act quickly.

This exercise won't make your mind up for you, but it will give you a broader range of options from which to choose.

Corporate personalities

When you're putting a business together, or trying to think of new ways to improve your products and services, one of the most effective techniques is to imagine that you've been bought out by another company or organization with a very strong corporate culture.

These companies have all been successful because they do one thing right.

By applying a range of organizations to your own problem you will at the same time apply their big learnings to your own problem.

Let's take an industry that hasn't shown an enormous amount of innovation – the shoe retailing industry. It's your job to shake it up and think differently about it. Now, as soon as I mentioned shoe shopping your brain presented to you all your experiences and assumptions about shoe shopping. It's very probable that mentally you're now sitting in a rectangular-shaped room with lots of shoes displayed around the walls and in the windows. There will probably be some seating in the form of benches in the middle of the room. There will be a back room full of boxes and the people serving you will probably be 16-year-old girls.

Now think what would happen if some big, successful and characterful organizations decided to get into shoe selling.

Organization	Core strength	Idea for shoe shopping
EasyJet	No frills but fun	$10 shoes you can change every week
Sony	High-tech	Computer fitting and making of shoes
Body Shop	Natural and ethical	Natural products, ethical manufacture
Disney	Child-friendly	Play area and branded shoes
The Army	Attack	E-mail reminders to buy new shoes
Boots	Health and beauty	Chiropody, reflexology, pedicure
Church of England	Tolerance	More sizes

A brand new idea

Imagine you had to write a personal ad for yourself in which the only means you had available to describe yourself were three brands. For example, if you wrote down that the three brands which summed you up were Rover, Pedigree Chum and Werther's Originals, everyone would have a pretty strong idea of what you were like as a person, and you can imagine what sort of person would be attracted to you (if any).

Try this yourself. What three brands would sum you up as a person? Think about food, drink, leisure, cars, cosmetics, clothing, etc. Most people find this exercise quite difficult, which is not surprising considering that you are a complex, multifaceted individual. It's also the case that all successful brands have a personality, a point of view and a perspective. Which is why you can use brands to give you a well-rounded and distinctive perspective to apply to a problem.

How to make engineering an attractive career choice by thinking about Volvo as a brand

Aspect of brand	Association	Idea for making engineering attractive
Safe	Job security	Promote employability of engineers
Reliable	Best kind of people	Advertise for people with 'the right stuff'
Big	Intimidating	Focus on niche specialities
Child-friendly	Flexible working	Flexible working and female-friendly
Swedish	Clean	Get rid of oily rag image
Sexier image	Hard hats	Encourage recruitment in gay community
Innovative	Richard Rogers	Play up link with design and architecture

Fresh mindsets

One of the major brakes on creativity in general is that people don't often get the chance to think outside their sector. How much fresh thinking are bankers going to bring to banking, or car retailers to car retailing, or computer designers to computer design?

To a certain extent, people who've spent some time in a particular industry become know-it-alls. Not in a bad way, because when you know a great deal about your industry it's natural to assume there can't be that much more to know.

Which is why it's always very refreshing when somebody from a bank takes over the Dome; or an insurance man takes over a supermarket; or a supermarket person takes over an airline. Almost always there is a new perspective and an infusion of ideas that may be old hat in one industry but are a breath of fresh air in the next.

It's the same cross-pollenization of ideas as from glass of water to cat food.

Put someone else's head on

Just imagine for a moment how a theatre critic would look at a yogurt.

They would be interested in the theatricality of the yogurt, how it opened, what sort of character it had, etc. Now imagine you were an architecture critic. You would now be looking at the yogurt in a different mindset. The structure would be more important to you, the marriage between form and function, style of construction, etc.

Newspaper critics are particularly useful individuals when it comes to importing other people's mindsets simply because every time they write a critique about something they use an abstract of the mindset of that profession.

Professional mindsets are very difficult to escape from especially if they correspond to the way you think about things naturally. For example, an actuary will always look at something in terms of risk and reward; a doctor will always be looking for symptoms of ill health; a guttering expert will always be keeping an eye on your pipework.

Try on one of the following critical mindsets:

Restaurant	Film	Football	Share price	Car
Ambience	Plot	Team	Mergers	Brand
Menu	Director	Tactics	Sales figures	Speed
Service	Cast	Opposition	Competition	Extras
Décor	Style	Ground	Markets	Design
Cost	Pace	Supporters	Technology	Space
Location	Editing	Stars	R&D	Safety
Wine list	Influences	Competition	Regulations	Cost
Clientele	Stars	League	Directors	Handling
Furniture	Interest	History	Dividend	Engine
Place settings	Effects	Pitch	Trends	Service

You now have a wealth of new perspectives and tools of analysis to bring to your problem or sector. If you haven't already done it, it's probably worth making a list of what things you notice about a problem or a situation first.

It's like paintings of a landscape. The landscape doesn't alter but the way it's perceived changes with everyone who looks at it. For example, when you've had a baby you'll notice that the world is full of babies. When you're an alcoholic you'll notice that the world is full of pubs.

thinking

innervation

momentum

When you're a creative individual you can shift your frame of reference at will, seeing all the possibilities and potential in any environment.

Or, as William Blake said:

To see a world in a grain of sand,
And Heaven in a wild flower
Hold Infinity in the palm of your Hand
And Eternity in an hour.

Auguries of Innocence

creativity part 1 – your slice of the pizza

We said we'd look at the part of the universe you don't have experience of first. By now you can see that it's possible and profitable to start your thinking anywhere except where it already is.

Earlier, I promised that we'd look at your own slice of the pizza. How your thinking is constrained by your own thoughts, experiences, understanding and knowledge and how these can all be used to better effect.

The first thing we need to talk about is language because all the stuff you have in your head has language attached to it.

Language – the words just come out wrong

You would have thought language would help us to think clearly. In fact it's one of the things that constantly gets in the way of fresh thinking. It's also a major barrier to effective communication but we can look at that in the chapter on communication later on.

Asking the right question

The first problem we have with language in our lives is that once we've verbalized a thought the words act like fast-setting plaster so that your original thought becomes a lot heavier, clunkier and difficult to change.

Many people have problems in their lives. Think of one you've got now. As you thought about it you probably formulated a sentence in your mind: How do I put my kids through college? How do I get a parking space at work? How do I fight this black dog of depression hanging over me?

In every case, the way you express the problem in language is part of the problem. Let me give you an example.

How do I spend more time in the garden?

Expressing your problem keeps your mind focused on the fact that you enjoy gardening and you don't feel you get enough time in the garden. But when I ask you what the question behind the question is, you may decide to express it in a different way:

How do I spend less time with my husband?

It becomes clearer what the real issue is, and in fact all your focusing on the garden was just a smokescreen. Let me ask you again what the question behind this question is:

How do I run off with Charlie Cheesecake in accounts?

Now we're getting somewhere. If you find yourself repeating the same old problem time and time again in your mind, chances are that you are asking yourself the wrong question. Generally, the reason you do this is to move responsibility for solving it away from yourself. You could quite easily solve the problem of spending more time in the garden by juggling round your diary a little, but that's not going to help you with the burning issue of your passion for Charlie Cheesecake in accounts.

This tendency to ask yourself the wrong question is particularly acute at work where the avoidance of responsibility has commercial implications.

Take someone who's continually asking herself this question:

How do I get my team to work harder?

A better question to be asking would be:

How do I motivate my team to work harder?

And the best and real question to ask herself would be:

How do I motivate myself to motivate my team to work harder?

Words and language are something outside yourself, and they often have the effect of distancing you from your thinking. You therefore have to be quite rigorous about the words you choose and you have to keep an eye on what they mean, if anything.

The power of clichés

Clichés are words and phrases that have been through the brains of a few people and the mouths of many. They are short cuts on the desk top of your brain. Clichés aren't born clichés. When the words are first minted they express a new truth or an old truth in a new way. The reason they catch on and become popular is because everyone recognizes their economy, effectiveness and freshness in expressing a thought.

Then, like an unspoilt wilderness, the tourist hordes trample underfoot the beauty that first attracted you to the word. Fresh words and phrases become clichés where only the ghost of the earlier meaning survives. Look at any corporate mission statement and you'll find them loaded to the gunwales with clichés.

Naturally, clichés have some usefulness otherwise we wouldn't all be using them all the time. But they are also dangerous professionally because they force you to think down the same tired and oft-trodden pathways.

For example, let's say you were a banker and I asked you to write down a description of your job in around 60 words which contained all the usual clichés. You might come up with something like this:

We aim to delight our customers and exceed their expectations, by supplying a one-stop shop of environmentally-friendly products and services, anytime, anywhere and anyhow, benchmarking against best practice to be a world-class organization. We will do this by empowering our greatest asset, our people, in an e-enabled, flexible and coaching working environment.

As a mission statement it's fantastic. There's probably something very similar in receptions of large financial institutions all over the world. If you look at the language you'll see that every cliché once meant something of value. But what they've all now lost is the ability to communicate, to cast a hook into the mind of the reader. So to all intents and purposes the above statement is useless because it doesn't say anything.

People know it's there, but they also know they know what it says, so they don't bother with it.

Now if I asked you to rewrite that 60 word mission statement for a bank using none of the clichés above (or any others that you missed the first time) it would be a lot harder. Why? Because you would be forced to think about two things:

◆ what the meanings of all these clichés really are, and

◆ more importantly, what it really means today to be a banker.

You might end up with something along these lines:

You know money isn't the be all and end all in life. You also know how important money is to do the things you want to do in life. You probably want to concentrate on holidays, education, getting a new car, paying for the house. We can help you with this – tell us how you want to manage your life and we'll help you to manage your money to make more of the good things happen.

By ditching the clichés you focus back on the meaning of bank. What is it actually there to do? Instead of focusing on the internal process (spending more time in the garden) you look at what the real issues are, what the customers want (Charlie Cheesecake).

Then as you strip away the old layers of meaning you might actually start to look at the biggest cliché of them all – banks. Banks have changed so much in the last 20 years why not call them something else? If you carry on the logic of your new mission statement they might be called money agents, or dreamworks, or facilitators or wallet or greenback or resource. The world is your lobster.

Good Lord

Here's one of the most eye-opening examples of the power of cliché to direct thinking. Take the Lord's Prayer with which most of us are probably familiar even if we don't give it much thought.

The Lord's Prayer 1	The Lord's Prayer 2
Our Father who art in heaven	O Thou, the Breath, the Light of all,
Hallowed be Thy Name	Let this light create a heart shrine within.
Thy kingdom come	And your counsel rule until oneness guides all.
Thy will be done	Your one desire then acts with ours
On earth as it is in heaven	As in all light, so in all forms.
Give us this day our daily bread	Grant what we need, each day, in bread and insight.
And forgive us our trespasses	Loose the cords of mistakes binding us, as we
As we forgive those who trespass against us	Release the cords we hold of others' faults.
Deliver us from temptation	Don't let surface things delude us.
And not into evil	But keep us from unripe acts.
For thine is the kingdom	To you belongs the ruling mind,
The power	The life that can act and do,
And the glory	The song that beautifies all,
For ever and ever	From age to age it renews.
Amen.	In faith, I will be true.

Imagine that a committee had decided to update the words to bring it bang up to date for the new millennium and the version on the right was what they came up with. Can you imagine the uproar and the letters in the papers complaining about the language being new age piffle and adulterating the meaning of the text, etc.

Now if I told you that the version on the right was a translation of The Lord's Prayer from the Syriac Aramaic, the closest existing version to the prayer that Jesus actually spoke, and was the version that was widely known and understood in the first rather than the third millennium AD, you'd probably have to do a bit of a rethink.

What this demonstrates, theology aside, is how our thinking and language and, therefore, our view of the world drift in and out of focus and alignment, and that continual refocusing, redefinition and rethinking is a must if we are to grip on our current reality.

Free extra – save your marriage

When you're next in marriage guidance counselling, look out for this really useful diagram.

What it shows is that at the start of a relationship we see people for who they are. Over time we build up an image of them. We seek out and then we start to relate to that image, looking for information that confirms what we think and disregarding anything that doesn't fit in. Pretty soon we lose sight of the complex, multifaceted person behind the image and, if they've been changing and maturing in different ways, they may not even be the person we used to know behind the image.

| The real fresh you |
| The real fresh them |

| The real fresh you |
| Small familiar bit of you |
| Small familiar bit of them |
| The real fresh them |

Save your marriage

It's the same with language. Get stuck in clichés and you lose touch with an ever changing reality.

Mission statements

Mission statements are the business equivalent of writing a letter to Santa Claus. If you boiled down the mission statements of the top 50 companies, what you would have left would be a lump of fat that read as follows:

We are committed to being world leaders in our industry. We will do this through delighting our customers by the world-class quality of our products and services. Our people are our greatest asset and we are committed to developing and training them. We respect the environment and are conscious of health and safety in everything we do.

What this means is:

We must make sure customers buy enough of our products to keep our shareholders happy. We will value our people as much as they are worth to us and comply with regulations concerning health, safety, environment, etc.

If mission statements are really to inspire, they should read more along the lines of:

We are going to be a fantastic place to work for three reasons:

- **we're all going to make loads of money because customers can't get enough of what we do;**

- **we're going to have an office environment that's just like home but without the children;**

- **we're going to rip the ass out of the competition and leave them for dead (or, for the public sector) provide an efficient and useful service to the community.**

Instead of missions, companies need concrete targets such as:

◆ we're going to market an electric car in four years;

◆ we're going to develop a legal mind-expanding drug in three;

◆ we're going to reinvent pensions in one.

Unrealistic? Try the Kennedy mission statement: we're going to put a man on the moon by the end of the decade.

Just imagine how the commandments would have sounded written like a mission statement:

We're committed to people living long lives and keeping their possessions. Parents will feel honored and we will have a culture of openness and honesty in which everyone will love each other. Oxen will be respected, etc.

It all sounds fine and dandy and not something you'd have any issue with. However, when it comes to rock solid commandments, it suddenly sounds a lot more challenging: Thou shalt not kill; Thou shalt not steal; Honor thy father and mother; etc.

That's why mission statements should take the form of commandments so that everyone knows exactly where they stand:

◆ Thou shalt meet thy targets.

◆ Thou shalt communicate internally at all times.

◆ Thou shalt take risks and think creatively.

◆ Thou shalt motivate and lead your team.

And of course, if you didn't shape up, you'd burn in hell-fire for ever. Mind you, if you're not doing these things already, your business is probably already burning in hell. If this is the case, you can always cheer yourself up by reading your company mission statement.

It's no surprise that the new economy has spawned a vast array of new language and new constructs because it really is a new way of thinking and doing business. One day all these new economy phrases will become clichés and then it will be time for free thinking and entrepreneurs to look for new words, new thoughts and new ways of doing business.

Six senses

Most of what we do requires language and business in particular is dominated by the written word. When you're required to communicate and think in writing the other senses get neglected. This is a big danger area.

If affection for a brand is the big differentiator then we need to use all six senses to promote it.

How often have you fallen in love with someone just because they write well? You fall in love using all your six senses: sight, smell, taste, touch, sound and your sixth sense (which I'm defining as the way you feel about something). Similarly, when you're innovating you need to think about all six senses.

For example, bank statements. For years they have been a piece of paper with words and numbers on them. In fact many banks didn't even bother giving you whole words, they gave you abbreviations which may or may not have meant anything to you, but they fitted the bank's piece of paper and that was what was really important.

Now some banks have woken up to the fact that for many people, their bank statement is the most regular form of contact they have with the bank and where they have direct, hands-on experience of the brand. Recognizing this, some bankers have refocused on the customer rather than the calculator and made their statements A4 size because that's the size our files at home are; they've designed them to be clear and easy to read; the entries are in long-hand and make sense of what, where and when the transactions were. There's even an opportunity for the bank to offer some helpful, tailored advice (cross-selling).

Emotional space – the sixth sense

Emotional space sounds like dreadful psychobabble about needing personal room to grow. In fact it's dreadful psychobabble about the intangibles around a product, service or person that add up to why someone likes something or someone.

Let's take smoking as an example. Many millions of people around the world smoke, even intelligent adults in developed countries who know that smoking gives you every disease in the book. So why do they do it? If you ask them this is the range of reasons they will give you:

◆ relaxation

◆ something to do with your hands

◆ keeps the midges away

◆ sociability

◆ extra breaks

◆ image – cool factor

◆ concentration

◆ appetite suppressant

◆ ritual.

Now some of these you would expect. People smoke because it gives them a buzz or helps them relax or concentrate. The image factor is a big one especially in getting young people started. But there are other ones that seemingly have nothing to do with the burning of tobacco and the delivery of nicotine. For example, sociability, extra breaks and something to do with your hands.

These factors comprise the emotional space round a product or person that helps build affection for it. A country post office isn't just where you buy your stamps, it's a social center, a first aid post, a meeting point and so forth and when one is closed it's the emotional space people miss, not the stamps.

Similarly, you may be surprised at why people like you. You thought it was your height and good teeth. Other people think it's the smell of bonfire you carry around with you and your unconscious humming of hymns. Brands have often been surprised by emotional equities they never knew they had. It's always a good idea to keep an ear out to what it is people really admire about you, your product or your business.

In the new economy, selling brands, services and yourself will increasingly require a greater understanding and appreciation of all the six senses including emotional space. Likeability – it's important in the playground, it's important in the new economy. Why? Because the new economy is a big playground.

Shaping and locating your problems

Although we're all brought up to think in terms of language and words and writing, there is a visual component in much of our thinking.

This is often a stronger barrier to creative and fresh thinking because we're not even aware of it.

Let me illustrate this for you. If you were to draw a map of where you went in life it would probably look something like this:

Home, work, home, work, home, work, home, work, visit supplier in Doncaster, home, work, home, work, home, work, home, work, home, visit friend in Swindon, home, work, home, work, home, go on holiday in Canaries, home, work, home, work, home, shop at supermarket, work, home, work, home, work, home, work, home, etc.

The lengths between each of the places may vary but not the width. By this I mean that you only see a slice of the world that is visible from the car or train window. And even if you're a globetrotter, you'll only be seeing the back of the seat in front of you, the lounge in the airport and your hotel room. These days, there's nothing like travel for narrowing the mind.

Spatially, can you imagine what would happen if you had to shift your entire life 100 miles across? It would of course be completely different and all the sights would be different and you'd start to get a

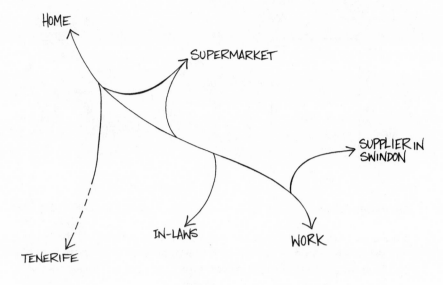

Map of life

whole new picture of the world. The same would probably be true if
you could shift it ten miles or even one mile.

Seeing things differently is a key skill in the new economy. People
who say no to new ideas usually say no because they just can't
picture it or because they're so locked into their existing view of the
world that they can see nothing outside it.

Take, for example, supermarkets. As soon as you read
'supermarkets', your mind delivered a lovely, fully-formed picture of
a supermarket, more than likely the one you visit on a regular basis
in the list above. Very probably it has a big car park, one entrance,
one exit and lots of aisles and rows arranged in H blocks.

That is the visual cliché of a supermarket. There are very good
reasons why they are laid out like that such as efficiency of customer
flow, maximizing use of floor space, etc. There's one thing you can
guarantee about supermarkets in the next 20 years and that is they
won't look like they currently do.

The winners in the supermarket wars will be those to escape the
clichés first. If we were about to reinvent supermarkets the first thing
we would do would be to tackle the visual clichés.

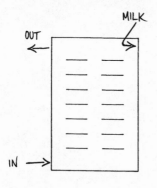

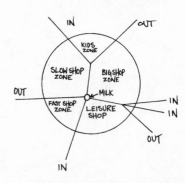

Supermarket cliché   **Supermarket based on map of Oxford**

Take a piece of blank paper and then draw a street map of the town or area where you live. You'll have roads, parks, motorways, schools, etc. Now imagine that the map you have just drawn represents the floor plan of the supermarket of the future.

You'll see already that there are leafy suburban areas and main roads. This gets you thinking about how this would apply to supermarkets: why not have slower areas where people who are really interested in what they're buying can take their time and make informed decisions? And then have a fast lane for everyday goods like milk, bread, etc.

Now apply all these new spatial features to the layout of your supermarket:

Map feature	New supermarket feature
Suburban area	Lifestyle leisurely food shopping on a winding trail
Roundabout	Central roundabout in store with different shopping segments
Several roads	Different entries and exits for different kinds of shoppers
School	A demonstration/education area for people to learn and try new foods
Park	A day-care center for children or male adults
Bypass	Fast lane for everyday goods
Shops	Specialist shops within the supermarket

By breaking up your visual cliché of what a supermarket looks like, you can free up your thinking on the whole area of supermarkets.

And don't forget to think in 3D.

Why are supermarkets on one level and department stores on lots of levels? There may be a good reason but there may be equally good if not better reasons why supermarkets should be on more than one level.

More spatial clichés

If you're reading this in a hotel, look down at the carpet. Isn't that the most disgusting carpet you've ever seen, apart from nastier carpets in other hotels. For some reason, hotels feel the need to have carpets designed like no other carpets: it's a spatial cliché of a hotel. If you're going into a hotel meeting room you'll find lots of spatial clichés. On the tables there will be little bottles of lime cordial. Why? Nobody drinks lime cordial in real life, why should they start in a hotel meeting room. Or mint imperials in little glass bowls. Or tables with felt over them. You expect to see these things so much in hotel meeting rooms that you don't realize how odd they really are.

Every space has its own clichés. Advertising agencies used to be considered incredibly avant-garde because they had sofas in their offices. You just don't expect to see a sofa in an office. In the same way you don't expect to see a swivel chair in your living room.

In business, there are many possibilities for innovation in mixing up spatial clichés. Banks and building societies suddenly cottoned on to this about ten years ago when they stopped looking like welfare offices and started looking more like travel agents.

Car showrooms are beginning to look less like a goldfish bowl with cars in and more like a living room with cars in. Dentists are looking less like surgeries and more like living rooms. Again the shift is from what you're doing to people in the space to how you're making them feel.

Organizing your problem spatially – drawing it, in other words

Often people like to draw out their problem in chart form or a little map of what's on their mind. The only disadvantage with this is that you tend to draw where your mind currently is and naturally you don't draw what you haven't yet imagined so your picture tends to be a bit fossilized.

In order to force our brains to think a little bit differently we can use the power of dualities. The universe is fundamentally in balance, that's why it and we can exist. The underlying balance in everything means that everything has two sides.

We know this in business from the phrases 'there's no such thing as a free lunch' and 'you get what you pay for'. In our personal lives we know the truth of the phrases, 'what comes round, goes round' and 'you get what you give'. Nature and the universe balance everything, however cleverly you may think you have tipped the balance in the short term.

Up/down	Real/virtual	Night/day
Left/right	Go/stop	Male/female
Still/sparkling	Light/heavy	Young/old
Black/white	Less/more	Poetry/prose
Cold/hot	Now/later	Full/empty
Big/small	Quick/slow	Right/wrong
Hard/soft	Fixed/mobile	Clear/opaque
All/one	Loud/quiet	Under/over
Flat/round	In/out	Here/there
Tight/loose	Micro/macro	Happy/sad
Open/closed	Town/country	Rough/smooth
On/off	Fat/thin	Rich/poor
Horizontal/vertical	Loud/quiet	Time/money

Dualities – the power of the dark side

Whatever thoughts you have, whatever you are, whatever property something has, there is always another side. This is the underlying yin and yang of the universe. Here are a few examples of the millions of dualities that underpin everything.

Take any problem you like and describe its features: then describe all the dualities. This is the dark undiscovered side of your problem, latent with potential innovation.

Air travel

Feature	Duality
Fast	Slow
Uncomfortable	Comfortable
Unhealthy	Healthy
Cheap	Expensive
Crowded	Exclusive
Characterless	Personality
Boring	Interesting
Impersonal	Personal
Above	Below

So where's the innovation relevant to air travel? Start with EXPENSIVE, EXCLUSIVE, PERSONAL. Clearly an airline that was just first class would be one way to go. Indeed some airlines are deliberately carrying fewer and fewer economy passengers to move themselves to the right of the chart.

But maybe the real innovation isn't to do with planes at all. Maybe it's to do with the revival of passenger liners. SLOW, HEALTHY, INTERESTING. After all, the cruise market is booming. People don't have a problem with big ships any more. They would be a lot faster than they used to be and with satellite technology you wouldn't be out of touch if you didn't want to be.

Or take this one step further. EXCLUSIVE, INTERESTING, BELOW. Passenger submarines. No seasickness, great views, etc.

Breaking up problems into delicious meaty chunks

Let's say a major dog food producer came to you and said we want you to think creatively about how to improve our dog food.

Where does your mind stray to first? Are you going to improve the product for dogs or humans? Are you going to look at price, promotions, packaging, distribution? Or are you going to look at taste, texture, smell, ingredients, nutritional values? Well, clearly you can look at all of them, but just by mapping out your problem into a number of different dualities you can get more than half way to a solution.

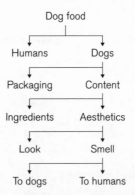

How to improve dog food

Solution
Make dog food smell good to humans!

There's a great idea – improving the smell of dog food for humans. And we got the idea simply by breaking down the problem into digestible, identifiable chunks.

Knowing what you know and knowing what to do with it

The new economy is all about information and knowledge, which is great. Having more information is good, understanding what the information means is better, but then applying this knowledge is best of all.

There is so much information in the new economy that knowing what you know is almost too much for any one person. Researchers are going to be very thick on the ground in the new economy. And the more researchers we have, the more knowledge we'll accumulate and the more research we'll need.

Increasingly, what will be really important is not the knowledge itself but the principles behind it. With an enormous amount of information available to everyone, the quality of your information will be less of an advantage. Advantage will accrue to the quality of application, and this comes back to first principles.

Let me show you what I mean. Imagine for a moment that you've just been made redundant but that a fantastic opportunity to manage a pig farm has come your way. You know nothing about pig farming (apologies to pig farmers reading this) but you've got to try it. Write down the ten golden rules of being a successful pig farmer.

thinking

innervation

momentum

Here's my attempt:

- have good pigs
- have enough land
- a good source of pig food
- breeding pigs
- good veterinary support
- market for your pigs
- transport to market
- skilled labor
- understanding neighbours
- detailed knowledge of EU subsidies

Now I know as little about pig farming as you do, but I wouldn't mind betting that the list provides 90 per cent of what you need to understand to be a successful pig farmer. Armed with those general principles I could find out the relevant information, skills and knowledge to implement them.

If I asked you to do the same exercise for ship-building, or running a theater company, or a sandwich delivery business, I know you could come up with the ten golden rules.

In the new economy you need to think first, use information second and always remember that information is no substitute for imagination, intuition and pure thought.

Pig farming may seem pretty irrelevant to you sitting there in your office in a big, multinational software company. But try this. You will undoubtedly have an issue currently in your in-tray which is either a communication issue, a team issue, a branding issue or an efficiency issue. It may have been lurking in your in-tray because it's a bit of a thorny issue and you're not sure how to tackle it.

Take a moment to write down the ten principles of good communication, or good teamwork, or efficiency or whatever the relevant area is for your problem. Do it for yourself and you'll realize that you generally have access to these golden rules. The problem is you have too much information and not enough general principles to guide you. Once you have the principles, apply them. They will give you a rigor, objectivity and structure to your management behavior.

You may have noticed that there are quite a few lists dotted around this book. They're all statements of general principles which then need to be applied in detail. Why do you think business books with rules sell so well? The seven habits, the ten rules, the 15 behaviors, the ten commandments, the 48 suggestions, etc. It's because people are looking for structures and patterns in the information blizzard to help them move through it without being blinded by information and events.

A big paradox

Everyone who writes a book secretly hopes they'll come across a paradox. They sound so intellectual for one thing. In academic terms they sound like you've discovered the secret entrance to a tomb.

Anyway here it is. Think of your current job: banker, IT specialist, brand manager, HR director, pig farmer. Then consider what the ten golden rules for being successful in your particular area are.

You know what the rules are and if you apply them rigorously and consistently, 90 per cent of the time you will be successful in your sector. But really big breakthroughs come about when you break the rules. Take for instance EasyJet. Up until then people had assumed that you needed to give food and drink and goodies on board a plane. EasyJet came along with no frills, but cheap tickets, and began to make inroads into the marketplace.

thinking

innervation

momentum

mapping the human heart

Two things that strategic thinkers, marketing people or anyone concerned with innovation always want to do is see the big picture and find the undefended hills.

Finding the undefended hills means locating those areas of the market that have yet to be exploited. There are precious few of these left so finding them is a bit like the search for the Holy Grail. Similarly, the rewards of finding them are equally satisfying. The other thing on the mind of marketers and strategic thinkers is something called the big picture. No one ever explains quite what this picture is or exactly how big it is. But one thing everybody agrees on is that having the big picture is a good thing. When was the last time you heard somebody saying we must have the small picture?

Over the years of brainstorming issues from pensions to pet food, and from condoms to cod liver oil, we have developed a technique that allows you to paint the big picture (no artistic talent required) and also to find where in the big picture those juicy undefended hills are. Of course, the undefended hills may actually be weaknesses in your own offering that are a big opportunity for your competitors. This is a way of plugging the gaps before they do.

We call this technique the **Map of the Human Heart**. The reason for the name is, firstly, because it attempts to draw a big picture of the entire range of emotions concerned in the purchasing and use of a product or service and, secondly, because the map itself looks a little bit like a heart. Well, more like a heart than a pancreas. The beauty of this Map of the Human Heart is that it can be used to analyze just about anything, any service and anyone you care to mention. We'll start by looking at a simple product, then a service, then a business, then a person and then finally at you, yourself.

So how do you put the heart together?

Start with a clean sheet of paper and draw a line down the middle. This represents the division of the world into Yin and Yang, that is the balance between the feminine and masculine impulses. Let me be quite clear here before the PC Gestapo knock at my door at three in the morning and drag me off for sensitivity training. We're not talking about men and women, we're talking about the widest possible distinction between the logical and the emotional, between the heart and mind, and between the functional and emotional. All the characteristics on both sides are present to a greater or lesser degree in both men and women, just don't ask most men to admit it.

The left-hand side of the map represents your rational reaction to things. In product terms it's whether you actually need something and, once you've bought it, whether it delivers what it says it will deliver (i.e., whether it does what it says on the tin). On the right-hand side you have your emotional reaction to things – whether you desire something in the first place and once you've bought it whether you continue to enjoy it.

We then draw a line across the middle of the paper that represents the event horizon or the continually moving dividing line between the present and the past. In commercial terms, the top half of the map now represents your first introduction to a product at the point of purchase. The bottom half represents your ongoing relationship with a product whether through usage or having the service related to it. In personal terms, the top half of the map represents first impressions – the ones you get when you first meet someone. The bottom half represents your ongoing relationship with that person.

That's how the map works in theory, how does it work in practice? Let's work through a couple of examples.

Example 1: buying a car

If you were simply buying a car to get from A to B you would be thinking purely in rational terms and presumably you would go out and get the cheapest car that would do that regardless of any other factors such as manufacturer, brand, handling, leather steering wheel, etc. My guess is you would end up with a fifth-hand Austin Allegro which has occasionally been known to get from A to B. Other purely rational factors when you go to the showroom include how many doors you're looking for (2, 3, 4 or 5), how much you can afford and how big an engine you want.

Nowadays, most manufacturers can cover all the rational decision-making factors, which means the emotional side of the decision-making process comes to the fore. For example, some people desire the new VW Beetle so much that all other concerns are secondary. They just have to have that car. Other must-have cars could be the new Mini, Dodge Viper, Fiat Multipla (it takes all sorts). In this emotional quadrant brand image and car design are everything.

Of course, people don't buy a car for just one day, they buy it with the next few years in mind (which is why drivers of hire cars behave so differently than when they are in their own car). Therefore ongoing functional factors, such as reliability, and emotional factors, such as enjoyment, are also equally important. On the reliability side you want to know that it will start first time, every time. You want to know that you won't be seeing daylight under the accelerator pedal because the rust is so bad.

On the enjoyment side there is how much you want to be seen driving the car. Do you blush with shame every time you open the garage door? Is servicing your car expensive, and a massive pain in the neck, or do they come and collect for you, leave you with a courtesy car and sort out everything without you needing to think about it?

Now you've got the map together you can begin to locate where various cars are. This of course is all personal opinion and you can make up your own mind. Japanese cars made their reputation entirely on the left-hand side of the map in that they were better value and more reliable than other cars on the market even if their brands were at first unknown. Even today, Honda is strong on the

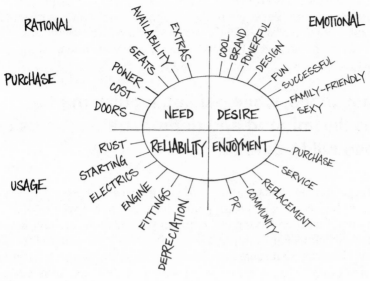

Cars

left-hand side and few people buy a Honda because it is the brand to be seen in. Interestingly, when Toyota wanted to go up market they decided to invent a whole new brand, Lexus, to move their position further to the right on the map.

Volvo also started on the left-hand side of the map, with a reputation for safety and reliability. As Volvo has become a global brand it has seen the need to have a more central position on the map and has made a conscious attempt to give the brand more emotional appeal. Hence the styling of Volvo has become more curved and less boxy, and the advertising has majored on driving and owning pleasure as well as safety, security and rigid passenger cells. That's why you now have advertising for Volvo featuring pictures of cars looking gorgeous but the line is 'Safe sex'. This is the Holy Grail of any great brand, which is to have your cake and eat it, i.e., claiming to have two seemingly irreconcilable features such as value and quality, or safety and sexiness.

In recent times, Korean entrants to the marketplace have found relatively few undefended hills to attack. Nevertheless, they've done so with considerable success. Firstly, they've worked on the principle that if you are the cheapest you can gain a certain share of the market and this they have done. Secondly, and more interestingly, Daewoo defined the market as enabling transport rather than just providing cars. It identified a gap in the market to do with servicing and ownership and revolutionized the way cars were bought and serviced.

Daewoo's innovations, while gaining it quick market share, were easily imitated and demonstrated the risk of having only one hill to defend.

Large global brands that maintain their successful position generally score highly across all four quadrants of the map. Experience has shown that even having one chink in your armour can have serious ramifications. For example, Fiat used to have a reputation for building cars that rusted easily. People don't buy sexy well-designed cars if they're likely to put their foot through the floor after driving through a couple of puddles.

Example 2: toothpaste

Razors, tampons, and toothpaste are three extremely high-margin products. Which may explain why there has been so much innovation and marketing behind them. Let's have a look at the map for toothpaste. If you're just looking for toothpaste that cleans your teeth, which does what it says on the tube, then you'll probably buy a supermarket own-brand toothpaste. Other rational decision-making factors are if you want a particular kind of toothpaste for kids or for smokers, or if you just want the cheapest. Toothpaste is a repeat purchase so you'll soon know whether a toothpaste is reliable or not: does it whiten your teeth, freshen your breath, protect your gums, etc.?

The more interesting side is the right-hand side and this is where the big investments happen. (As a general rule the more mature the market for products the more innovations and investment tend to be directed to the right-hand side of the map.) Think of the reasons you buy your toothpaste if it's not for the rational reasons above:

◆ maybe your parents bought that brand;

◆ maybe you like the stripes in it;

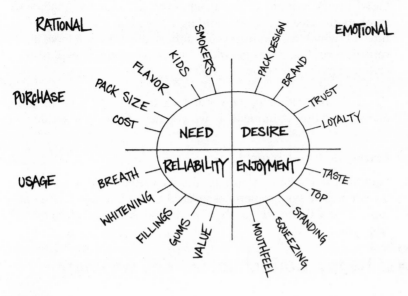

Toothpaste

◆ maybe, thanks to years of advertising, you recognize and trust that brand.

The big question for toothpaste manufacturers is whether you'll continue to buy that brand and this comes down to the ongoing enjoyment of using it. Do you like the taste, the colour, the smell (can you remember what your toothpaste smells like)? Do you like the way it squeezes? Is it a major engineering operation getting the last bit out? Does the tube have a snotty nozzle or does it have a lovely clean action? Can you stand the tube on its head or is it a wrinkled metal coil sitting in the soap dish?

If that's the map of toothpaste, where would you innovate in it? Well, for a start you could import some brand values. For example, if Chanel developed a toothpaste it would leave the other toothpaste brands standing in terms of bathroom brand presence. Mouthfeel has been an area of innovation: baking soda toothpaste gives you a more interactive and exciting feel in the mouth which makes you imagine something rather vigorous is happening in the cleaning department.

Or why not combine nicotine patches with smokers' toothpaste so smokers can clean their teeth and fight their craving at the same time. Or why have toothpaste in a tube at all? Why not have it in capsule form that delivers exactly the right dose in an explosive charge right in your mouth?

I'm just making these up now, but it's a lot easier to think about how and where you can innovate when you have the map to guide you.

Example 3: high street bank

Banking used to be very simple. You gave them your money, they gave it back to you, sometimes with a little bit extra. If you spent more money than you had they would take a little bit extra away from you.

Everyone was happy. Correction, nobody was happy.

Apart from the banks, which made a lot of money for very little effort. That's all changing now because the banks have competitors on every side and for the first time they've been forced to address the total Map of the Human Heart and start thinking about having a warm relationship with customers.

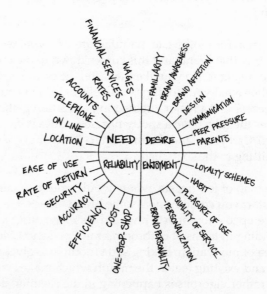

Bank

Exercise 4: your partner

Getting closer to home now, you can map out your relationship with your partner, your boss or even your local butcher if you thought that would be a profitable use of your time.

Concentrate on your partner for the moment and by this I mean your life partner, not the person you share your legal practice with. The top half is when we meet our partner, the first impressions if you like. Now most of us, before we meet our partner, are usually carrying around in our head a template of what our ideal partner should be like. Tall, dark and handsome is the most clichéd of templates but you can also include the fact that you would expect him or her to be from the same part of the country, or the same ethnic background, the same age bracket, or the same sexual orientation. These are the rational filters we use when selecting a partner and, if you have an arranged marriage, will be pretty much the only criteria used.

Partner

In our western, romantic culture we believe that the emotional side of the map is important in finding a partner. That's when things like humor, personality, firm buttocks, etc become more important.

That's the chemistry we believe is important in attracting people to each other and often works in completely the opposite direction to the rational side. Someone once said that the heart has reasons of which the mind knows nothing (possibly Jack Welch).

Now if we stopped there we would be talking about a one-night stand. But relationships often last longer than that and what then becomes important is how the two of you work together or get along together. On the rational side is how you work together as an economic and social unit – your faithfulness, your earning power, your fertility, your sociability. On the emotional side is whether you continue to emotionally satisfy each other, which has to do with comfort, communication, sexual satisfaction, friendship, cold feet in bed, etc.

If you map out the different affairs, partners and spouses you've had, you'll see where their various strengths and weaknesses were.

Passionate affairs tend to concentrate on the right-hand side while happy marriages, like the Ford Mondeo, are strong in all four quadrants.

Example 5: you

The Map of the Human Heart applies to you as the person equally well as to toothpaste. I know that's a little bit depressing because we all think of ourselves as being slightly more emotionally and functionally sophisticated, but in fact it would be pretty simple to draw the map for an average working person and then locate yourself on it.

In this case, the top half of the map will represent your first meeting with another person. This can be in an interview situation, a sales presentation or simply in the first meeting you have with someone. Clearly, in the new economy where you're working with a greater range of people, you're going to be in a situation where first impressions count much more often. Although it's not a classical interview situation, it might as well be because people are making similar sorts of judgements based on similar sorts of criteria.

In business, people sometimes refer to candidates for a particular position as being 'job ready'. What this means is that they fall into the top left-hand quadrant completely. They have all the functional attributes necessary for the job. They fit the template. And let's face it, if you don't fill these boxes it doesn't matter that you've got all the charm in the world because you're not even going to get the first interview.

You in the new economy

Out of the smaller number of people who are 'job ready', the person who goes the furthest will most often be the person who scores highest in the emotional quadrant. That's the box where people decide if they like you or not. Or, more importantly, where you try to make people like you.

If you've been on the receiving end of interviews and have never actually interviewed someone yourself, you may be under the false impression that there is some kind of science behind them. There isn't. Or at least there may be but towards the end of the analysis someone always starts talking about a gut feeling. All this really amounts to is whether somebody likes the candidate or not.

One person I know had the interview technique of a chair leg. Although she was very good on paper and physically not disgusting (it's important and you know it's important) she just came across as a cold fish and all the members of the interview panel couldn't foresee themselves enjoying working with her. However, one person had the courage of his convictions and had somehow managed to see something in her that nobody else had. This may be because he had a personal recommendation from her previous boss. In the event she was hired and after a while became the managing director of the company. But you can see how close she came to being handicapped by not scoring high enough in one quadrant.

Know your undefended hills

If you map yourself on this chart you probably won't be surprised at where your strengths and weaknesses lie. On the other hand, you may be more surprised if you get somebody else to map *your* strengths and weaknesses. Very often they're not where you think they are.

Once you determine where your own undefended hills are, there are two things you can do about it.

The first is to try to fill the gap. This isn't as easy as it sounds because it's difficult to manufacture being a charming, entertaining individual when naturally you've always been a slightly shy introvert. If that is the case then it's important to compete in those areas in which you have strength. For example, if you are interested in an IT job, the fact that you are better qualified than anybody else weighs a lot more heavily than the charm you have. Similarly, if you are on for a sales job and you know less about the product, it's probably best that you concentrate on the soft skills side.

Your ongoing relationships in business are not simply a question of scoring highly in box 3. These again are the table stakes required for anybody who wants to get on in business, ie reliability, flexibility, self-motivation, a responsibility, and efficiency. What makes a difference is what happens on the right-hand side. What decides people about whether they like working with you all comes down to whether you are seen as a sociable person, someone with humor, someone who knows how to have fun, somebody who can be trusted, somebody who listens, and is generally an all round good egg.

Often this is referred to as your emotional intelligence and it's a vital thing to have in the new economy.

It's especially vital when the thinking is over and it's actually time to do something.

doing

innervation

moment.um

be your own boss

You're not going to get anywhere in life or in work if you're not your own boss. Before you hand in your resignation, buy a second-hand van and start selling integrated network solutions door to door, I should make it clear that being your own boss doesn't mean that you have to work by yourself for yourself. You can have bosses stretching away to infinity and still, to all intents and purposes, be your own boss.

Today's organizations have structures so flat you can see to the horizon. You may see your line manager every day; more likely you see her once a week. Or maybe you have several people to report to or you work for yourself in your own business. You may be any of these things, but in future we're all going to be working for ourselves, managing our own businesses or part of the business even when we're in a multinational organization with thousands of employees.

When we talk about bosses we're talking about a new kind of boss. Someone who makes his own decisions, executes them and, incredibly, takes responsibility for them.

Old economy bosses

If you're not your own boss, somebody else will be and we all know about old style bosses. The difference between an old style boss and a high street bank is that banks occasionally give you credit for things.

Bad old bosses think that what they do is to boss people about. They give you things to do and then blame you for doing them. As an added bonus they tell you NOT to do something and then ask you why you haven't done it. Finally, to motivate and encourage you, bosses then claim they can do your job standing on their heads. This may explain why, for a lot of the time, they seem to be talking through their backsides.

These are bosses whose personal self-esteem rests on the size of their company cars, how near their parking spaces are to the front door, memberships of golf clubs, size of desks, etc. They're mostly men, they're mostly in their fifties and if they have a bright future, it's in a well-lit cabinet in the Museum of Office Dinosaurs.

These kind of bosses always claim that they have a lot of responsibility and that 'the buck stops with me'. To their minds this is an American phrase meaning that the vast majority of the payroll stops in their wallets. They believe in performance related pay only as far as they'll give you a pitiful raise and if you make a performance, they'll take it all back.

For most people, boss trouble doesn't come from the Chief Executive or Managing Director. It comes from the person who's promoted one micrograde above you and overnight becomes General Pinochet in boxers. Suddenly, whatever you are empowered to do, he is empowered to undo.

That's because for some people getting a promotion at work has strange physical side effects. Firstly it changes their eyesight so they suddenly see what a load of good for nothing shirkers the rest of the team are. It also lengthens their wind so that they take up 10 per cent more air time in meetings. After getting a promotion these people try to prove they deserve it by becoming Business Nazi of the Year for the next three months until they realize that the rest of the team have all handed in their notices.

In the real world, bosses like this exist. If you are one, then get out of the way of all the talent and ambition you're thwarting.

If you have a boss like this then he is a major obstacle to you being your own boss and doing your own thing in your own way. Remember, the acid test of a good boss is whether you're learning something from him and that doesn't include learning to print out your CV when he's not looking.

Manage your bosses better than they manage you

When you work for an organization under someone else, the key to being your own boss is to manage him better than he manages you, so you maintain freedom of decision making and action in all the vital areas. This is how you do it.

Do your job without bothering them

Ask any boss who they would consider the ideal person to manage and nine times out of ten he would say someone who doesn't need managing. If you can get on with your job with the minimum of fuss and give him the required results without massive collateral damage, then it's more than likely that you will be, in all senses that matter, your own boss.

Keep them informed before not after

Anyone can be self-managing for a week, maybe even two. Some people can get away with it for months at a time. But then there will come a crisis, good or bad, that requires your boss to be involved. If you then convene an extraordinary meeting for the purposes of communication, it's going to be the first they've heard of the crisis. They won't know anything about the background to the issue, the key people, the key points. This will make them panic. They will feel in the dark, adrift and, worst of all, pressurized. That's why they will give you a hard time, make the crisis seem worse than it is, and generally charge around with their asses on fire.

All this unpleasantness can be avoided by continual ongoing, informal communication. Just dropping by your boss' desk, or seeing her in the corridor and letting her know what's going on, has all sorts of benefits:

- It keeps your boss abreast of the situation and gives her something to say when her boss asks her how things are going.

- It covers your back so that you can always say, 'I told you about that in the corridor.'

- It gives good bosses a chance to sniff out any potential problems before they detonate.

- It gives you a chance to relate to her as a human being (see below).

The key thing is getting into the habit of informal communication with your boss. This means that when important things happen not only do they get communicated quickly but, ideally, they can be done informally without the need for convening a formal meeting for the purposes of communication.

Unleash the power of gratuitous flattery

This doesn't mean getting into the habit of congratulating your boss on tasks that could be done by a small monkey. The secret of really effective flattery is to congratulate your boss on how good a manager he is. Deep in their hearts, senior managers are often as surprised as you are that they are in senior management.

I know the thought of saying to your boss, 'You did a good job there, Brian', gives immediate rise to the following feelings:

- you feel slightly uncomfortable

- you feel slightly creepy

- you feel a bit of a hypocrite

- you feel a little bit like throwing up.

Of course, we'd all rather not do it but just put yourself in his shoes for a moment (and can I just say what excellent taste in shoes you have there, Brian). Imagine you're getting an absolute roasting for accidentally deleting the company Intranet. Come on, we've all done it. Just wait until the shouting is finished and then say, '*I admire the way you managed me there, Brian*.' It doesn't have to be Brian, obviously.

Ask for the benefit of their experience

The most effective form of flattery in all situations is to give someone your undivided attention. When managing your boss this translates as asking for his advice to benefit from his greater experience. It's no good waiting for him to come round to your office, perch one buttock on your desk, and then lecture you for half an hour on the golden days of business in the 20th century. This is a classic example of managing your boss better than he manages you. Pick the time that's suitable for you and then ask him for the experience.

The result of asking for advice and then listening attentively is fourfold:

◆ you make him feel as though he's helped and everyone wants to feel that

◆ you understand a bit better the way he thinks

◆ you might actually learn something

◆ your ass is covered as you asked for his advice.

Remember the names of their children

Senior management can be quite a lonely job and, to be fair, the amount of responsibility does increase. Most senior managers feel a real sense of responsibility for the people who work for them. Treating your boss like a fellow human being, a colleague, even a friend, makes her life and yours a great deal easier. But don't ever expect to be bosom buddies because, in the last resort, if someone's got to fire you, your boss is going to be the person who has to do it.

That said, there are some shortcuts to friendliness and sociability that are worth taking. Remembering the names of the boss' children is one of them. Obviously, if you haven't remembered your boss' name yet, you might want to make that your starting point. He might not have children either. In that case, you need to go to his desk and see what photos are on it. If it's a TVR Cerbera then ask about that, if it's a small dog ask about that, if it's a photo of you, worry.

Invite them out for a drink or lunch

There's something about asking your boss out for a drink, or even a spot of lunch at the pub, that facilitates most of the above rules. You seem like you're being friendly, you're communicating informally, you're giving him your undivided attention and you're out of the office hierarchical environment. Avoid expensive restaurants or the hierarchy stuff will kick in again over who's paying.

Lunch

Lunch is an enormously powerful management tool and will get more and more so. People increasingly want to do business in an informal setting and there is no better constructed occasion than lunch.

Breaking bread with someone has a mystic significance.

It's neutral ground. You're away from technology. Who pays is important. You can cement the relationship by saying 'The next one's on me'.

doing

Starters	Small talk	'How's your cat?'
Main course	Context setting	'Have you noticed the sales dive in apricots?'
Dessert	Problem solving	'Perhaps we could repackage them.'
Coffee	Next actions	'I'll give you some research budget and we'll look into it.'
Paying	Gratitude expression	'This one's on me. You've really helped me out.'
Taxi	Kiss	*You're confusing a business lunch with a romantic dinner.*

innervation

(If you're doing the main information giving it doesn't matter what you order because you probably won't get an opportunity to eat it.)

momentum

Never invite your boss round for dinner. It's your home and you shouldn't be bringing your work home. You don't want him to come round and he doesn't want to come round. Just keep chatting to him at work. That's enough.

Help them do their jobs

Although it's difficult to credit at times, your boss has a job to do as well. You're a key part of doing that job. What you need to do is make sure you understand what his key tasks are, what he's being measured on and the part he expects you to play. You could be wasting a lot of your time doing something that is of no importance to him.

Once you understand what's driving her, you can adjust your effort accordingly, always remembering that there should be more to your job than keeping your boss happy. There are other small but significant factors like customers and innovation to be keeping an eye on.

The principle of helping your boss is an important one and applies equally to customers (who should be your real bosses). Customers have jobs to do or lives to lead and they will appreciate you more if you appear to be making both easier. You don't want to be going up to people and saying, 'How can I improve your life today?' but you get the drift.

Give them solutions not problems

In the old economy people didn't talk to their bosses and when they did it was because there was some monstrous cock up that needed sorting pronto. When you're continually communicating informally this won't be a problem as potential difficulties will normally be headed off at the pass.

But changes do happen, problems arise, challenges rear their ugly little heads. Instead of running off to the boss and saying look what I've got for you, there's always the option of solving it yourself. Or at least having an idea of how to solve it and taking the possible solution to your boss (or customer).

Again this gives the boss thinking time, shows you're on the case and covers your bottom.

Give yourself another key task

Asking for more work is the modern equivalent of asking for more food in a Dickensian orphanage. But that's how jobs grow, one responsibility at a time. If you can take responsibility for a small part of your boss' job, you have already promoted yourself for the proportion of his job that piece of work represents. Your boss is also grateful to you and is obliged to you in some small way.

It goes without saying that you shouldn't be volunteering to take on work when you're already on the brink of a nervous breakdown from overwork. Nor do you want to take on work that you can see no future value in. By future value we mean work which will bring you credit, earn you money, teach you something, or raise your profile.

Get promoted above them

There are two types of ambition in business:

◆ one is to build a global company from scratch and become a billionaire before you're 30;

◆ the other is to get a 5 per cent salary rise and a company car.

The first kind of ambition is usually easier and a lot more fun because you can waste your whole life trying to get an extra 5 per cent from someone whose own ambition in life is to stay precisely 5 per cent ahead of you.

Ambition is a bit of a dirty word in business.

To say in a meeting that you're very, very ambitious is like going on a date and saying you're very, very randy. It may be true but saying either is unlikely to get you what you want any quicker. On the other hand, saying you're not ambitious in business is the equivalent of saying that mentally you have already taken early retirement.

In the good old days of jobs for life, ambition was a simple matter of stepping on the head of the person beneath you to lick the shoes of the person above. In the new economy, promotion is generally a matter of moving sideways, or to a different company or growing your own job. There are no dead men's shoes and if there are, you wouldn't want to fill them.

doing

innervation

momentum

In business, we all know there are no problems, only opportunities. The reverse is true in promotion appraisals. When you're offered a big opportunity look out for the big problem. Never, ever fall for *'We're giving you a big promotion but your salary will remain exactly the same.'*

Now you're on your own. Or are you?

Once you are able to do your own thing in your own way, once you are operating as your own boss, you will find that you still need help and support to achieve things. That's when you have to start thinking about teams.

How to manage your bosses better than they manage you

◆ Do your job without bothering them

◆ Keep them informed before not after

◆ Unleash the power of gratuitous flattery

◆ Ask for the benefit of their experience

◆ Remember the names of their children

◆ Invite them out for a drink or lunch

◆ Help them do their jobs

◆ Give them solutions not problems

◆ Give yourself another key task

◆ Get promoted above them

teams are for fantasy football

I always get suspicious when I hear companies or old style bosses talking about teams. Have you noticed that the Sunday papers never have a list of Britain's richest teams? And you don't often get team leaders saying, 'It's a team Porsche and all the team can have keys to it.'

People talk rubbish about teams: a popular phrase and something that I've seen up on someone's wall as a motivational poster is, 'There is no "I" in "team".' Perhaps it would be rude to point out that there's no 'we' in team, there's no 'you' in team, there's no 'them' in team. But there is an 'i' in 'after dinner mint'. So where does that leave us? Nowhere.

The thing is, if you're going to be in a team, you might as well be the team leader. Because, as the old Yukon saying goes,

If you're not the lead husky the view never changes.

Old economy teams

In the old economy, everyone was put in some sort of team. Every so often, just to prove they were all a team, the team leader would call together the team for a team talk. This is where the leader would talk to the team, get its feedback (both positive and negative) and then rebuild the team minus anyone who said anything negative.

This is what they used to call teambuilding.

There was another form of teambuilding in the old economy. This was when the team leader got together a group of people who didn't work very well together in the office, took them out into the country somewhere and then put them through a series of mental and physical exercises, that all proved that the team didn't work very well together outside either.

Let me ask you a question. Has anyone reading this book, in any job they've ever done, needed to cross a river on an oil drum, three planks and a length of rope? Of course you haven't.

A more useful exercise would have been how to keep smiling when you're being shat on from a great height. We all need to know how to do that.

Old style teambuilding could be fatal for team leaders whose credibility as a team leader would disappear the instant the team saw them for the first time in jeans that looked as if they were part of the uniform for the Greek Navy.

The worst part of this kind of teambuilding was so-called trust exercises. This involved standing on a piece of concrete, closing your eyes and falling backwards *trusting* that you'd be caught by a colleague whose annual holiday you'd just cancelled. You actually learned a lot about trust. Especially when you closed your eyes, fell backwards and then opened them again in an intensive care unit.

What you really learned is that trust in business is something you have to earn, teams are something you have to build yourself, and leadership is by inspiration, example and first-class management.

In sport, teams play against each other. In much of the old economy, teams within organizations played against each other. Arbitrarily selected teams then demanded loyalty to an artificial creation that served neither the business nor the customer. Teams, departments, silos and fiefdoms (call them what you will) locked in information, people and customers. They were badly selected, badly managed and badly led.

New economy teams

If I asked you to write down the team you work in, more often than not it would be the team you had been given to work in; the team that fits on your company organizational chart. The sales team, the IT team, the Midlands team, etc.

Now if I asked you to write down the team without which you couldn't do your job, it would look very different:

◆ it would include suppliers;

◆ it would include customers with whom you have a really good relationship;

◆ it would include people from other parts of the business who help you out.

Perhaps you have somebody in IT who helps you adapt the system specifically for your needs; or someone in logistics who doesn't mind a bit of fresh thinking about how things get done; maybe you have a mentor, formal or informal, who you can bounce ideas around with; perhaps your partner at home gives you good ideas and advice; or perhaps he gives you the motivation you need for the job. Or what about the person you used to work with, who's now moved to a different company but who's still in touch?

Recognize these people? That's your team for the new economy. What they have in common is that you have a good relationship with all of them, you trust them and they're willing to help. That's the definition of a working team. There are no artificial boundaries, no first XI, no team uniform. The team adapts and reconfigures according to your needs at any given time. It's a virtual team. It's a team you've picked from the best players wherever they happen to be sitting, living or working. That's why teams are for fantasy football.

Picking yourself for a team

We borrowed the old economy notion of teams from the Japanese. At the time, the Japanese seemed to be working together a whole lot better than we in the West were. So we imported as much as we could of their consensual, non-hierarchical, self-less teamworking ethos.

What we forgot to import were two additional elements that made this approach work for the Japanese.

◆ Firstly, the 4000 years of cultural development that subordinates the individual will to the common good in Japan.

◆ And, secondly, and probably more importantly, we didn't really pick up on the fact that Japanese teams are extremely carefully selected so that they are composed of a set of complementary skills such that each person being in that group adds to the synergy of the whole group.

To the Japanese, the notion of having all the same type of people in a team would be ludicrous. It would be complete duplication of people and effort. To their way of thinking, if you are not adding something unique to the team you shouldn't be in it. That's also a very good rule for the new economy. If you're not adding something of unique value to any team you feel part of, you shouldn't be in it, because there's no doubt that it will be filling your life full of unnecessary meetings and drabness.

Leading a team

The best thing about the Japanese way of putting teams together is that everyone in it knows they are a vital part of it. Similarly, with the fantasy football teams of the new economy, where everyone selects their own team to do the job in hand, there's only one team leader and that's you. It doesn't matter what official team you're in, it doesn't matter where you are in the old style hierarchy, if you've picked your own team then it's up to you to lead it.

There is no such thing as a good team without a leader.

It's like having a good car without a steering wheel.

The five types of leaders in the old economy

Before we think about how to lead a team in the new economy we should look at the five models of leadership in the old economy.

Autocratic leaders – got somewhere but they didn't take anyone with them

Everyone's come across this type of leader. They're bright, they know where they want to go, they know all the strategy. But basically they're a playground bully. They get their way by shouting, by ordering, by sacking, by vicious office politics. These were the dominant beasts in the old economy jungle.

Democratic leaders – took everyone with them, but they didn't get anywhere

A slightly later development in 20th century management. Very sensitive and aware people with very advanced personal skills, but no grasp on strategy, vision and tactics. You couldn't want a nicer person to let you know that the company was going into receivership and that you'd lost your job.

Charismatic leaders – nobody got anywhere but everyone felt terrific

These were leaders who had so much charm and charisma you would follow them anywhere. The trouble is they tended to move faster than you could follow and what they left behind them wasn't worth staying for.

Bureaucratic leaders – only the paper got anywhere

All the personality of a hub cap but very effective in that they had a stranglehold on the movement of paper and, very often, money. Generally from an accountancy background, they were most happy when closing down the entire company to make cost savings.

Cheer leaders – a lot of smiling and fancy footwork but not actually playing

When getting on in business was about your old school, playing golf with the right people and being clubbable. Fantastic motivational work on their annual visit to the shop floor though. Not really leaders at all. More pub bores.

In the late nineties there was a hot new management style in leadership based on something called *coaching*. At the end of every millennium people have a nasty feeling that the world is about to end and decide that it's time to improve their behavior. Coaching was part of this. At its worst, it was how consultants charged for teaching people basic good manners.

New economy leadership

Ironically, the new economy model for team leadership is taken from a very traditional source – the army.

When you're in the army in a fighting platoon you have something called the point man.

This is the soldier in the front line, who's leading the patrol into enemy held territory. He's the first to see what's happening, the first to meet the enemy, the first to take new ground and the first to hoist new flags over conquered cities.

Point leadership

The most important thing about point leadership is that it is leadership from the front. What does that mean in business terms? It means different things depending on what you're doing for a living. It can mean dealing with customers, everyone knows that they are the front line. But it can also be on the front line of technological innovation. Let's face it, with technology, if you're not on the front line, you're not really innovating. It can mean anything or anywhere where changes implemented will alter the big picture. And that can include operations, marketing, finance, HR. The important thing is that you are leading these changes that move the company forward.

Point leadership comes from the front not the top. That's because customers notice leadership from the front, never the top. When was the last time you heard a customer say, 'I'm getting shoddy, overpriced goods with appalling service, but I don't mind because you've got such a strong board of directors.'

Bringing your teams with you

The point man in the army can only concentrate on moving forward if he is absolutely confident of one thing and that is covering fire. He must know that the rest of the team is behind him, that they're following him. They know he's taking the lead, but they're backing him and they will go with him wherever he leads.

Now think of your own team. Perhaps it's the team you've been given, the team you've picked or, most probably, a combination of the two. How do you lead a team like this?

How to be a point leader

Passionately believe in your vision

There's no point in having a team if you don't know what you're going to do with it. Not only must you have a clear goal, you must be passionate in your belief that it's worth doing and worth doing well. Enthusiasm is a great persuader and a great motivator. You can't blow an uncertain trumpet. So decide what you're doing and give it your best shot.

Build a team that shares your vision

You don't have to have a team full of people who are as passionate and committed to your vision as you are. You shouldn't expect it either. If they're the kind of people you want on your team they will probably have their own ambitions and priorities as well as being supportive of your own. It's a very rare team where everybody is completely unified and single-minded in purpose.

Tell your team exactly what you expect of it

The best basis for leadership is mutually understood expectations. Agreeing expectations, exploring assumptions and setting goals at the beginning of any enterprise is absolutely critical, whether it's manhandling a piano up a spiral staircase or putting a woman on

Mars. When people are absolutely clear where they're going and what part they are expected to play in the journey, then leadership becomes a matter of a light hand on the tiller rather than continual wrenching efforts to keep everybody on track.

How to communicate effectively with your team

◆ Tell it like it is

◆ If you really believe it, show it

◆ Listen before you think before you speak

◆ Headlines first, then the whole story

◆ Consistency is the clearest message

◆ If it really matters, do it face to face

◆ Involvement is the best persuader

◆ Encourage feedback and act on it

◆ Little and often is better than long and loud

◆ Communication works when something changes

It's so critical in fact that I'm going to repeat the last paragraph.

The best basis for leadership is mutually understood expectations. Agreeing expectations, exploring assumptions and setting goals at the beginning of any enterprise is absolutely critical, whether it's manhandling a piano up a spiral staircase or putting a woman on Mars. When people are absolutely clear where they're going and what part they are expected to play in the journey, then leadership becomes a matter of a light hand on the tiller rather than continual wrenching efforts to keep everybody on track.

Listen to your team and respect its skills

A common mistake in leading a team is that a great deal of care and attention is given over to selecting the team in the first place and agreeing roles but then what happens is that the leader tries to do everything herself. There's no point having a dog and barking yourself. You've picked these people for what they can do. Let them do it. There's probably a whole range of other things they can do about which you had no idea when you picked them. Let them do those as well.

The key is listening (see the chapter on communication). Keep your ears and your mind open to what your team is telling you. And if they don't tell you, ask. Expectations, assumptions and directions change continually. You need to keep listening continually to make sure you are still on the same wavelength on all three.

Keep everyone informed and motivated

The other half of the communication equation is the fact that your team, to a greater or lesser extent, volunteered to work for you. That means they probably value what you have to say and are hoping to learn something from you and from their jobs. Keep people up-to-date on your own thinking and aspirations. If they haven't changed, just tell them they haven't and that your enthusiasm is undimmed. Also tell them about your job: what the challenges are, how it's going, how they can help.

Work harder than anybody else

Tricky one this. It doesn't mean working yourself into an early grave. It means that if you have built a team to deliver your particular vision, whether that's better customer service, a new system, faster operations, a whole new product – whatever it is, it's your baby and you should be seen to be doing the lion's share of the work.

Of course others will be working hard but don't forget that they'll also have other things that are closest to their hearts. Expect commitment but don't expect everyone to be quite as committed as you. The upside of this is that when people see real commitment and effort from the top, it tends to inspire effort and commitment from the rest of the team.

Very occasionally be ruthless

Things don't always go to plan. In fact, when it comes to things actually happening, the one thing you can be absolutely sure of is that they won't go according to plan, no matter how hard you worked at the planning.

Normally, your vision will remain the same but the route you have to take to get there will change. Often events change faster than people. You shouldn't be surprised at this. Obviously there are some people who don't want to change, but more often than not the situation requires a change in one direction and they're predisposed to change in another direction.

This is normally not a major problem unless the vision and the goal of you and your wider team are threatened by the inability of that person to do what is required of them. If you've followed the above rules they will already be clear of the changed situation and the reason behind it. They will also have been made clear of how expectations and tasks have changed. If they didn't buy into it then, or they refuse to buy into it now, they must be axed. Given the chop.

However much we've coached someone, nurtured them, communicated with them, listened to them and so forth, there may come a time when you and they have got to part. When it comes to this, if your conscience is clear (and it will be if you've been straight with them all along) then cut them out quickly and cleanly. Any delay will hurt you, hurt the project and won't do them any good either.

Incentivize everyone

Keeping everyone motivated is vital to get the best out of people. A large proportion of keeping people motivated is treating them decently as a human being. A little human kindness and consideration goes a very long way. I've known people give up the working ghost for want of a simple thank you. It may not mean much to you, but boy does it mean a lot to other people.

The most important part of motivating someone is to understand what motivates them. This may well be a thank you for work well done. It may be continual mental stimulation. It may be continual customer contact. Generally, it will be under the banner of job satisfaction. People are satisfied in different ways. Find out what it is for each individual.

Of course, there are a tiny, tiny handful of people who are motivated by money. Well actually it's a rather large handful. We're all motivated to a certain extent by money. We work to live and some of us are lucky enough also to enjoy our jobs. Yet it is very rare that money is the sole motivator for people. There are some exceptions to this: people often go into banking, accountancy or the law for no other reason than they are likely to earn a good wage. Good luck to them. They have made a conscious decision to be motivated by money and shouldn't therefore complain when their jobs are unrewarding in other ways.

Share the rewards

Once you've understood the range of people's motivations you can share the rewards more effectively. Sharing the rewards often means sharing out the profit. Performance related pay works, especially when it is on top of a reasonable basic salary. Commission only jobs tend to dehumanize the individuals involved as they are measured on nothing but sales.

Sharing the rewards can also mean sharing around the other good stuff in work; for example the travel, the events, the training or the perks. Again it's all a matter of what motivates you. One person's perk is another person's occupational hazard.

Give the right training and space to grow

Well motivated people will move mountains. But no amount of motivation will help you do something that requires skills. Give your team all the training it needs and as much as it shows an interest in. Remember that learning something is one of the key ways people measure job satisfaction.

And finally, let them get on with it.

How to be a point leader

◆ Passionately believe in your vision

◆ Build a team that shares your vision

◆ Tell your team exactly what you expect of it

◆ Listen to your team and respect its skills

◆ Keep everyone informed and motivated

◆ Work harder than anybody else

◆ Very occasionally be ruthless

◆ Incentivize everyone

◆ Share the rewards

◆ Give the right training and space to grow

doing

innervation

momentum

off-line networking

Listen very carefully to your boss when he talks about teams and make sure that what he is really talking about is not **My Little Empire**. If you want to be an imperial civil servant fine, then keep your attention fixed upwards and see if you can do your job in your own little silo, department, fiefdom or whatever you want to call it.

In the new economy you shouldn't be in any team that isn't helping you to do your job better. To get the job done in the new economy, you've got to be a **free trader** in who you talk to, who you work with and who you share ideas with. Find interesting people and work with them.

That means networking.

Networking sounds as though it would be a pretty important skill to have in the new economy. It is. But you have to be very clear about what sort of networking you're talking about. We're not talking about any sort of IT network or the Internet. These are absolutely core to the whole concept of the new economy and whole books (many of which are intelligible) have been written on the subject.

The kind of networking we're interested in is how to meet, pick and sustain the kind of teams based on a loose collection of individuals required for any given job. This is a long way from the awful, debased networking of the past.

Networking in the old economy

Old style networking was based on having a vast number of business cards which you gave out to people you met in golf clubs. This kind of networking was named after the old Network South East. It was a waste of time and money and there was no guarantee you'd get anywhere.

You'll know someone is an old style networker because they'll give you their card within the first 30 seconds of a conversation. After about two minutes of telling you how brilliant they are, ask them whether they would like your card. As they couldn't give a monkey's about anybody else's card, why not give their own card back to them and watch them slip it straight back in their pocket.

At parties, old style networkers talk about 'working a room'. You'll know them because, while everyone else in the room is enjoying themselves, they'll be the ones working like stink. Their aim is to ask everyone in the room what they do and dump them after three seconds if they're not useful. To networkers the person over your shoulder is always more interesting than you are. Overall this creates exactly the same impression as if they'd walked round the room handing out cards saying 'I am a loser.'

If these people waited for someone to *ask* for their card, they'd still have a full deck. The reason why they're always handing out their card left right and center is because they believe it's not what you know, it's who you know. What they don't realize is that you can know 6000 really useful, powerful people, but if every single one of them thinks you're an industrial-strength idiot, you're not going to be going anywhere fast.

Networking – the hard way

Getting things done in business as in life is simply a matter of making sure you speak to the right person. Sadly, the right person doesn't normally exist and 90 per cent of the time you have to make

doing

innervation

momentum

do with the ignorant, lackadaisical half-wit who has the intelligence and initiative of a hub cap and who single-handedly seems to be causing a slow-down in the economy.

Somewhere in a mythical land far, far away is a person:

◆ who knows exactly what you're talking about;

◆ who has your information at their fingertips;

◆ who can do exactly what you require;

◆ who can do it immediately and seems to take a genuine pleasure in serving you.

If you ever, by some miracle, come across such a person, you tend to be so pathetically grateful that you actually forget why it was you called and instead start thinking about finding out who they are and marrying them. It goes without saying that when you call them again the following day, they will have ascended into heaven and some new half-wit will be attempting to help you by accidentally wiping your records off the computer.

Occasionally you get so cheesed off with the customer service assistant you're speaking to, you attempt to escape them by asking to speak to the supervisor. Remember that the supervisor has been trained to use the phrases 'I can appreciate', 'Let me take your details', and 'We're making every effort' in any combination they see fit in order to pacify you.

Never ever get angry with supervisors.

Apart from the fact that it won't get you anywhere, you should remember that you only have to deal with the original half-wit on this one occasion, whereas the bonus of the supervisor depends on his performance day in day out.

The right person

At the same time, you have to remember that everyone in their own particular way is the right person for something. Everyone has either the experience, the program, the form, the docket, the knowledge or the key to make something happen in the easiest manner possible. But then the next immutable law in business is that when anybody wants to do this particular thing the last person in the universe they will ask is the person who could make it happen. Had they but asked, everything could have been done and dusted in seconds. But they don't and so they have to reinvent the wheel, take the driving test and do a couple of crash tests while the person with the easy solution is standing patiently at the finishing line. In this way, everyone has to learn to do everything from scratch. That's what they mean when they talk about a learning organization.

Networking in the new economy

What you know about who can be useful is necessary if you're going to be Machiavellian about things, but real advantage comes from something else. In the knowledge economy the real key is knowing who knows what and knowing what you know already. Continually extending what you know through knowing other people with different skills is what's really important. Building a reputation as somebody who can get things done by selecting and applying the right people with the right skills to any given problem will get you a long way further than the dentist's waiting room.

In the end, all business success depends on relationships. And with all relationships you get what you give. So when you're thinking about networking – think about what you can give, not what you can get. If you develop the mindset of continually asking how can I help this person – be they a customer, colleague, boss, subordinate – then you will develop a group of people who will continually share their ideas and concerns with you because they know you will listen and are there to help. And when the time comes to actually ask them for something, you will find yourself well in credit in the favor bank.

Networking requires meetings which, if they're done like they've always been done, is very bad news.

Meetings in the old economy

When you wonder what you've been doing with your life for the last few years, you can look through your old diaries and realize that you've actually been in a meeting.

In the old days, in big companies, half of every working day was spent in meetings, half of which were not worth having, and of those that were, half the time was wasted. Which meant that nearly one-third of business life was spent in small rooms with people you didn't like, doing things that didn't matter. The only reason people had so many meetings was that they were the one time you could get away from your work, your phone and your customers.

Most meetings were spent either talking about problems arising from work that hadn't been done or talking about work that needed to be done to tackle problems. There were so many of these meetings that there was very little time to do any work or solve problems which meant only one thing – more meetings.

Generally, there is no such thing as an interesting meeting.

That's why nobody ever comes out of a meeting saying, 'Wow that was a fantastic meeting, let's have another one now instead of going home.' You can judge how tedious meetings are by the doodles they generate. Anything that looks like the product of a spider on speed means you're probably in the worst of all meetings, the status meeting. These are so-called because everyone tries to prove their status by talking loudly about their own achievements.

Meetings in the new economy

Meetings are still absolutely vital in the new economy because people will be networking, building their own teams and building businesses. In fact, meetings will be more important than ever because all these things will have to be done faster than ever. The difference is that nobody can afford to have long, pointless meetings that suck the marrow out of precious working days.

Running a short, effective and enjoyable meeting is one of the core skills to have in the new economy.

Decide what kind of meeting you're having

Meetings fall into the following four categories.

Selling

This is where one party is selling or presenting to the other party. These are the most formal of all kinds of meetings, in structure if not in content. There's a definite opening, main pitch and close.

Information sharing

These meetings, sometimes called status, progress or production meetings, are all about servicing and maintaining an ongoing relationship or project. They happen regularly and their format varies little from one meeting to another.

Problem solving

Rarer than other meetings, these require that thinking be applied to a problem and actions on it decided. Often very amorphous in structure, they can take a very long time. They would benefit most from more structure.

General chit-chat

These meetings are often accompanied by food and drink where you just maintain the personal relationship and listen to each other's concerns and aspirations.

Why meetings are so often a waste of time is that people confuse what kind of meeting they're in. If you've got a problem to solve there's no point wasting time with a lot of social chit-chat. Similarly, if someone's relaxing over a drink with you they might not want a sales pitch.

Be aware what kind of meeting you're going to have (set expectations if you can) but also be aware that successful meetings are generally a combination of all four. At the beginning and the end of the meeting there should be time for general chit-chat. This is to relax people and to give them a chance to air what's on their mind outside the more formal agenda.

doing

innervation

momentum

Information sharing always happens so that people can bring themselves up to speed on what's been happening in the business. This will require some active listening and questioning.

At some point in the meeting someone will want to sell something. By this I mean 'sell' in the loosest possible way, in that they will want to put forward an idea for something new and will attempt to persuade the meeting of its merits.

Once the sell has been made there will often be a problem-solving session where the way forward is worked out and any obstacles overcome.

Plan exactly what you want to achieve

It's only possible to have a successful meeting if you know exactly what you want to get out of it. Your goal doesn't have to be earth shattering – getting to know somebody better is a legitimate outcome for a meeting. If you don't have something specific you want to get out of the meeting, don't have the meeting.

Only invite people you really need to be there

Meetings are like church services in that once you're in one you can't then stand up, shout that it's all rubbish and then walk out. There's nothing worse than being in a meeting to which you can contribute absolutely nothing. It's a squanderous waste of time and an equally steep opportunity cost. (You've lost the opportunity to be doing something else that's much more worthwhile.) People who realize that they shouldn't be in a meeting will be extremely disruptive as they will do anything to shorten proceedings and get out.

The general rule is that the more people you have in a meeting the less likely it is to achieve anything.

When you go on a week's holiday you miss on average ten meetings, but curiously nobody misses you. That's because meetings have a life of their own regardless of the people in them. Don't go to meetings out of habit. Only go if they're really going to be useful to you or you're going to be really useful to them.

Let people know what the meeting's about

You're more likely to get the right people in the meeting, thinking in the right way, if you make clear what the meeting is about beforehand. This gives the chance for people to include or exclude themselves and to give the points on the agenda a bit of thought. It also means you too have to give the points on the agenda a bit of thought, which is no bad thing.

Prepare an agenda for the meeting

People say that the secret of a good meeting is preparation. But if people really prepared for meetings, the first thing they would realize is that most are completely unnecessary. In fact, a tightly run meeting is one of the most frightening things in office life. These are meetings before which you have to prepare, in which you have to work and after which you have to take actions. Fortunately, these meetings are as rare as a sense of adventure in the finance department. One of these meetings in January is generally sufficient to give a medium-sized company enough momentum for the whole year.

Write yourself an agenda for every meeting and make sure you cover all the points.

Start and finish on time

Time in meetings is always different from real time. A quick, ten-minute catch up can fill a whole morning. One of the reasons for this is that work in meetings doesn't actually start until someone says, 'I've got a meeting to go to.'

People will be more likely to come to your meetings if they know they start and finish on time. Many people have back-to-back meetings and keeping them waiting will throw out their entire day. (More fool them for having back-to-back meetings.)

Be aware that people's stomachs are more powerful than their minds.

doing

innervation

momentum

If you say you're going to finish for lunch at one, nobody will be listening to a word you say at ten past one especially if they can hear crockery chinking in the background.

Respecting other people's time is the cornerstone of building a good relationship with them. Why should they do anything for you if you keep them waiting?

Introduce everybody to everybody else

You're never going to have a successful meeting with someone when you don't know their name. Make it your absolute priority to find out and remember everyone's name. People's names are very dear to them. They want you to know what it is and to get it right. It also makes doing business over the phone a hell of a lot easier.

Manage egos and control airtime

Meetings where there are more than four people encourage those with large and unwieldy egos to go into display mode. For example, when there is clearly a need to problem solve they will still be in information-giving mode, often at high volume and at great length.

These people need to be controlled and the best way of doing it is – as we've said before – to have stated up front what the purpose and structure of the meeting is. Stick to the agenda and beware of hijacking. If you've called the meeting, you must get what you need out of the meeting. If other people want other things, let them call their own meeting.

Agree who does what and when

Never finish a meeting without getting closure on who is going to do what and when they're going to do it. This is the vital setting of expectations for the next part of the business process, whatever that is, and can range from organizing the Christmas party to invading the European mainland.

Networking is as simple as having a constructive conversation – and as difficult. So difficult in fact that the whole of the next chapter is devoted to one subject – communication.

communication – across the great divide

What separates us from the animals is our use of language. A shoal of a million fish might not be able to write Romeo and Juliet between them, but they can change direction as one in the blink of an eye. Using language, a human team leader can give an instruction to a team of six people and have it interpreted in six completely different ways. Language has made complete communication and understanding all but impossible between people.

Nevertheless, when you're a grown-up adult, trying to earn a decent living, you're going to have to accept the fact that you'll be dealing with people. You therefore have two choices:

◆ either you become a hermit, writing advanced code for computer software in a darkened room somewhere;

◆ or you learn to engage with other people, to communicate with them, understand them and influence them.

I should warn you now that writing advanced computer code is the easy option. That's because people have far more sophisticated code than computers and they also have legs so you can't mess up their programming without expecting them to walk away.

Communication is the tip of the iceberg

Given the vast number of thoughts and feelings we all have about so many subjects, any form of meaningful communication really is a minor miracle. What we say is really only the tip of an iceberg of feelings, knowledge, experiences and culture.

	Mary the Director	**Ian the Manager**
COMMUNICATION	'That report needs writing'	'Yes, the client asked for it yesterday'
ASSUMPTIONS	You're writing the report	You're writing the report
	I'm giving you an order	We're having a chat
	It's client A	It's client B
	It's the IT report	It's the HR report
	You're not very busy	You're not very busy
	You're that Ian	I'm the other Ian
RESULT	Nothing now, shouting later	Nothing now, pain later

When we share many experiences and assumptions with someone else, you'd think communication would be easier. Sadly, that's not always the case as communication within families can be an absolute nightmare as I'm sure we've all experienced. On the other hand, when you meet a stranger from a strange land, communication can often be relatively good, because neither of you will be making any assumptions that you understand the other person and where they're coming from.

In our normal, hurried western world, most communication is like ships that pass in the night. You have a rough idea that something's out there, but you haven't got the time, energy or interest to get the detail. Some people say that the secret of friendship and personal relationships is good communication. In reality, we are most relaxed and happy in our relationships when we don't feel the need to explain and argue and communicate all the time. When you're on exactly the same wavelength as someone else you can finish each other's sentences, you say the same things at the same time and you can communicate volumes by the raising of an eyebrow.

With most people we have to work a lot harder to get our message across and to understand what they're trying to say.

Language is what we use to communicate between individuals. Language is also the major obstacle to communicating between individuals.

That's because words have no fixed meanings, and nor do the sentences that carry them. We use words to simplify complex thoughts and inevitably a lot gets lost in the translation.

Our consciousness is limited to roughly seven bits of information at any given point yet our unconscious stores every breath we've ever taken, every thought we've ever had. No wonder communication is such a partial, tenuous business.

So what is effective communication?

Communication is attempting to transfer a thought from one person to another. This isn't a one-way process. You could be broadcasting great thoughts night and day, but until they are lodged in someone else's consciousness, you haven't communicated anything. Talking at great length and at great volume isn't communication, it's junk mail. Real communication is like registered post. For communication to be complete not only must the thought have arrived intact in someone else's brain but the person who sent it must acknowledge receipt.

In communication terms, what is evidence of successful delivery? It's the response you get. Try saying 'I love you' to someone who doesn't respond at all. The first thing you'll assume is that they haven't heard you; the second is that they don't understand you; the third is that they don't love you. At this stage, the only thing you can be sure of is that your communication has been a failure.

Instead you could get the following responses:

1   I'm sorry, what was that?
2   Que?
3   So you love me, do you?
4   I love you too, let's get married.
5   I'm still giving you this parking ticket.

Responses 1 and 2 show your communication has failed. Responses 3, 4 and 5 show successful communication. Only response 4 shows successful communication and successful outcome (a bit too successful some might say).

Often people will not respond to your communication in the way you expect. That's not their fault, it's yours. They're responding to the way they understood your communication, not the way you meant it.

It's your responsibility to make yourself understood.

In communication, understanding is everything, intention is nothing. The real meaning of communication is the response you get.

How people talk

If you want to improve communication it helps to understand how people talk and how they listen.

Some people think then talk

There are so few of these people that they're usually mistaken for some kind of prophet or Messiah. When was the last time you were struck by the originality and perspicacity of something someone said to you?

Some people think as they talk

Most people don't know quite what they think until they've said it. As they can't think as fast as they talk this means lots of talk and not much thought. This is the main reason why meetings take so long.

Some people just think

These people are so rare that they get confused with people who don't think or talk and are written off as being completely stupid, which is a bit of a waste really.

Some people just talk

These people are just noise in search of a thought. You don't really listen to these people, you just have them on in the background, like daytime TV. There are an enormous number of people like this around who talk incessantly just to keep themselves company. There's nothing wrong with this in its place (a sound-proof cell) but when you're attempting to communicate properly and get things done, these people must have their airtime rationed.

How people listen

They don't

Sadly, it doesn't normally matter how you talk because most people aren't listening anyway. How often have you asked, 'What was I saying?' and realized that the other person hasn't got a clue?

When you think people are listening what most people are doing is waiting politely until you've finished so they can start. A clue to this is how often they say, 'yes'. That's a little signal that tells you that 'Yes, I know what you're talking about and can you please stop so I can air my far more interesting and urgent thought'. Thanks to this style of listening, most conversations are actually two beautifully dovetailed monologues.

You can't listen and think at the same time

Ironically, as soon as you say something interesting, people will stop listening and start thinking. It's like throwing a stick for a dog; as soon as you've thrown it, the dog's off. He doesn't want to hear your reasons behind the throw before he goes and gets it.

People listen for rather than to

When people are listening to you they may have their ears open but their minds closed. They've already made up their minds what they think and they're only listening for supporting evidence for what they think or a hook to introduce what they think and want to say.

Ears have springs

Their natural position is closed or, more correctly, they are on standby. They can hear things all the time but they're not processing. For this you have to make an effort to start listening and then further effort to keep listening. Listening properly is hard. It takes a certain amount of self-control to stop your mind wandering and to really concentrate on what someone is saying, especially if it's completely familiar or completely unfamiliar.

Given the double whammy that people don't think before they speak and that people aren't listening anyway, it's not surprising that communication is our number one problem.

When things go wrong in business it soon becomes clear that everyone thinks they did the right thing and the fault was actually in the communication. Of course, the wonderful thing about communication is that it's a no-man's land for blame as everyone either meant the right thing or understood the right thing.

doing

innervation

momentum

Good communication

Speak in headlines

When you know how ineffectual most people's listening skills are you can adjust the way you speak in order to accommodate this. People can only keep their ears open for a very short time before they are distracted by their own thoughts and what they want to say. The way to tackle this is to talk like a newspaper. Start what you want to say with the headline thought. This is what has to grab their attention, to invade their thoughts and to get them into receive mode.

Once you've got their undivided attention, you can then move onto the rest of the story and as much detail as they want. If you want to communicate your opinion about Scottish devolution you should start with the headline and say, *'The Scots should be independent.'* If you start by saying something like, *'They're a funny old lot the Scots,'* the other person is more than likely to start thinking about their own interpretation of why it is that the Scots are a funny old lot before you manage to get your own view over.

Listening as a martial art

If we're brutally honest there's something a teeny bit wet about listening. It's what marriage guidance counselors do. It's a little bit passive, a little bit submissive. It's not something red-blooded, ass-kicking business types do. It's true enough that many red-blooded, ass-kicking business types don't listen but then who wants to spend their whole business life with their foot attached to someone else's backside.

Listening is active not passive. If you want to be butch about it, you can destroy someone by listening to them so closely that all their weakness, hypocrisies and inconsistencies are mercilessly exposed.

At its most powerful, listening and silence can draw vast egos into the void and cause them to explode because of the sheer force of their internal contradictions.

That makes listening sound a bit better doesn't it?

More constructively, you can listen intently to someone and completely understand their plans, worries and aspirations. At the end you will be better informed, and they will feel hugely motivated and understood.

After sitting next to Mr. Gladstone I thought he was the cleverest man in England. But after sitting next to Mr. Disraeli I thought I was the cleverest woman in England.

Princess Marie Louise, Queen Victoria's granddaughter and early admirer of Jack Welch

Don't just sit there

The key thing to remember is that listening actively doesn't mean sitting there silently with a soupy look on your face. There are four separate but vital stages to listening.

Turn on your receiver

You need to make a conscious decision to put your mind into receive mode. This means opening your ears and equally importantly closing your mouth.

Tune in the signal

You should be aware when somebody is talking to you that they are making a host of assumptions, many of which you will not share. You therefore need to use who, what, why, where, when and how to continually check the meaning of what they're saying. You don't have to turn your listening into a Gestapo interrogation, you just need to clear up any misunderstandings and ambiguities as you go along.

Also be aware that many people ask questions that are not really questions at all. In fact they're just their points of view and opinions dressed up as a question. The most common method of introducing one of these so-called questions is with the phrase, 'Yes, but don't you think that blah, blah blah ...'

Turn up the volume

When you get to a part of the conversation that you consider to be the nub of it, you can home in on that and amplify the signal if you like. Try some of these phrases to do this:

◆ Tell me more about that.

◆ What's the thinking behind that?

◆ Let's drill down into that.

◆ What do you mean by that?

◆ Can you unpack that for me.

◆ Really? (with sincerity)

Record and play back

This last stage of listening is the proof of the pudding. It doesn't seem like listening because what you're actually doing is talking. What you do is play back your understanding of what has just been said to you. This is one of the most powerful techniques you can use in business and personal relationships.

Why? Because if you know you're going to feed back at the end of listening, it's a huge incentive to concentrate on what people are actually saying. You're going to look pretty stupid if you feed back something that bears absolutely no relation to what's just been said.

Nine times out of ten the process of playing back what somebody says gives rise to clarification, either because you genuinely got the wrong end of the stick or because they genuinely gave you the wrong end of the stick. At the end of a conversation or business meeting, playing back what has been agreed is a great way to finish the meeting and get agreement on exactly what everybody has communicated.

The other beauty of playing back what somebody has said is that they genuinely feel they have been heard. Even if things don't go their way, at least they feel they have had their say and feel they have been listened to.

Finally, after the trauma of having to listen to somebody else's opinions without prejudice for a good few minutes, feeding back gives you the chance to talk and the feeling that you're back in control of the agenda.

Establishing rapport

There's a lot of common sense about establishing rapport with people and there's also a lot of very highbrow pseudo-psychological stuff that goes under the general umbrella of Neuro-Linguistic Programming (NLP).

Common sense first

◆ Body language is important when you're listening to somebody. If you look relaxed, they will relax.

◆ You need to get at their level so that you're not towering over them or making them feel inferior.

◆ Don't cross your arms. This just makes you look aggressive and defensive at the same time.

◆ If you're sitting at the table, avoid sitting with the table between you as this distances you from the other person and makes you appear more officious and less sympathetic.

◆ Maintain as much eye contact as possible without appearing psychotic.

◆ Don't take notes unless you've got shorthand. You can't listen properly while you're mentally composing the notes you're making.

◆ Make clear that you have time to listen. People won't open up if they think you're about to rush off.

Neuro-Linguistic Programming

There's a whole science attached to the art of communication – NLP. This breaks down the way people communicate into three main groups: visual, auditory and kinaesthetic.

◆ **Visual** people tend to see the world in pictures and use words which reflect this.

- ◆ **Auditory** people tend to hear and read the world in words and their language echoes this.

- ◆ **Kinaesthetic** people tend to experience and touch the world and their language has the same feeling.

Once you've identified the sort of person you're dealing with, you can create rapport with them if you mirror the way they talk. So when you're demonstrating something to a visual person you say, 'Let me show you'; to an auditory person, 'Let me tell you'; and to a kinaesthetic person, 'Let me give you a feeling for this.'

It's a nice theory but not very practical. Most people are a mix of all three types and language certainly is, if you see what I'm saying. Or hear where I'm coming from. Besides which, if you're concentrating on how people are speaking, then you're probably not listening to what they're saying. It's a bit like literary critics who can tell you all about the use of language in a novel but can't tell you what the plot was.

Gluteal communication

If you've already paid thousands of dollars to go on an NLP course, then let me introduce you to the advanced version. There is a fourth group of people, mostly male and mostly in business, who are gluteal in the way they communicate.

Talking through your ass

You may think that the most potent and popular concept in business is money. It isn't. In fact it is something much closer to home. It is the humble ass and business is full of them.

A stupid ass is someone who chooses to do something idiotic whereas a silly ass is someone who does idiotic things because they simply don't know any better. Tight ass refers to anyone who has a fanatically clean desk, never buys a round and generally looks like they're sucking a pickled onion. A smart ass is anyone under 30 who works in IT. Pains in the ass are widespread in business. A pain in the ass is someone who is so often a pain in the neck that he becomes a permanent ache lower down the spine.

In the office there really is no legitimate excuse for assing about. When you're assing about and make a mistake you may well find your ass in a sling. If you go on making mistakes you may find that your ass is on the line and that your boss (or pain in the ass) gives you a serious talking to and warns you to get your ass in gear. It's important not to get assy at this point or you may well find yourself out on your ass. Of course if you really can't be assed to listen to your boss having a go at you, you can always take the high-risk option and tell him to stick it up his ass.

If you want to get ahead in business you need to get off your ass or simply get your ass moving. The one exception to this is if you happen to be the rare kind of person who actually has the sun shining out of his ass. Unless you are constantly illuminating a stream of people behind you, it's usually best not to claim this for yourself. If you do, there's a real danger that people will think something equally remarkable is happening, and that you're talking through your ass.

Having an ass is not necessarily a bad thing in the business world. The trick is to know your ass from your elbow and not get the reputation for being the sort of person who wears their ass for a helmet. This avoids the embarrassment of getting things ass about face, going ass over tit and generally making a right ass of yourself. Finally, you shouldn't try to be too clever in business as this in turn runs the very real danger of you being accused of disappearing up your own ass.

Once you realize just how important the ass is in business, it will come as no surprise to know the overriding concern for most people in business at all levels is to make sure their asses are covered.

Communicating to large audiences

Apart from violent death, most people fear public speaking more than anything else in life. Professional entertainers actually refer to disastrous performances in public as 'death' because you're standing in front of a group of people who look as though they're watching your coffin being lowered into the ground.

When you're in front of this kind of audience you often wish your coffin was being lowered into the ground.

However, most people in business will be called on to communicate what they're doing to an audience at some stage. This may be three people in a meeting room or 3000 people in a conference room. Here's how to do it.

Getting started

A presentation is like a poster beside a motorway. It has to communicate one clear, bold message, and it has to do it first time. Therefore, the first thing to do is ask yourself, 'What is it I really want to say?'

Then ask yourself:

◆ Why do I want to talk about it?

◆ Why will the audience want to listen?

◆ What is the one thing I want them to remember when I sit down?

Next, produce an outline of what you want to say on a single sheet of paper. Begin by setting out your message. Then, briefly, sketch out a theme or conceptual framework to convey that message. Follow this by outlining, in order, the points or arguments you believe put your message across most forcefully. Under each point or argument, set down the best selection of information, facts and statistics that will help drive home the message.

Generally, you should tell your audience what you're going to say, say it, and then tell them what you said. But you should also keep them with you by using phrases such as:

'I'd now like to talk a little about ...'
'Let's now move on to ...'
'As I mentioned earlier ...'
'Wake up you bastards ...'

Close a presentation the way a pilot lands an aircraft. First, signal your intention to land; then land; and then tell them what to do now the flight's over.

Above all, keep your presentation **short.** It's always good to remember that nobody is as interesting as they imagine they are.

With presentations, less is always more.

We live in a sound-bite age of information overload and short concentration spans. An hour is a very long presentation. Aim for 25 minutes of closely argued, action packed, easily digestible, useful and relevant information.

A few notes on style

In all presentations follow the KISS rule: Keep It Short and Simple. The optimum time for a presentation is about 20 minutes. One page of double-spaced large type equals roughly one minute's speaking time.

If you are planning a presentation that is substantially longer, you must have a rich and varied menu of audio-visual support. You must also make doubly sure that the structure is crystal clear and that your audience knows from the word go exactly what ground is going to be covered.

Speak, don't read

Ideally, you won't write down your presentation. You'll have a few notes or PowerPoint slides and you'll talk from them. If you have a clear structure in your head, you'll be able to talk naturally and cogently without hesitation, deviation or repetition.

Now, I know this is a tall order and most people prefer to have a written presentation, especially if they're facing a large audience. Just remember when you're at your PC typing away that presentations are written to be **heard**, not read. Write in the active rather than the passive voice, ie 'We must communicate better', as opposed to 'Communication must be better'. As a rule of thumb, the more you use the words 'you' and 'we' the more likely you are to keep your audience engaged.

Don't use words that you wouldn't use in conversation. Break grammatical rules if it makes your meaning clearer. And there's nothing wrong with using 'and', 'but' or 'because' to begin a sentence. Worry about understanding, not about grammar. Short sentences are best. They work. Use them.

Humor is a very useful way to help establish a rapport with the audience. But if you're not naturally funny, don't make jokes. You will, as comedians say, 'die on your ass.' The best humor arises naturally out of the subject matter.

88 per cent of statistics are meaningless

Avoid statistics. If your presentation is packed full of statistics you might as well send a letter. Statistics should be used to make single powerful points. For example, 'Our success rate is 98 per cent. That sounds pretty good. But if Heathrow air traffic control's success rate was 98 per cent there would be seven crashes a day.' Up to the minute facts and personal references help a presentation seem fresher and more alive.

Kill your babies

When you're writing your presentation, you need to be hard on yourself. If you think something is particularly witty and clever, make sure it's not also self-indulgent. As they say in advertising, 'Kill your babies.' If in doubt, leave out.

Visual support

Slides and visual aids can help make a good presentation even better. They can also ruin a good presentation, and make a bad presentation buttock-numbingly dull.

Slides will help you make your point if they are simple, uncluttered and underline the point you want to make. Too often, people pile on the information in their slides, thinking that the more information they put over, the better the presentation. That's a big mistake.

Keep the information to a minimum. Two or three points are all an audience can take in while you're talking. If you have a complex point to put over, build it up over two or three slides. Never, ever turn spreadsheets into slides. They will be worse than useless.

Allow **a maximum** of one slide per minute of speaking.

Photographs, cartoons, diagrams, bar and pie charts – anything truly visual – will help you make your point more effectively than plain numbers or words ever will.

When you are preparing information for slides remember that they are landscape format rather than A4 portrait format. Never put information on a slide that has no relevance to what you are saying in the presentation.

Video – big bucks, low impact

Having video inserts can give you and your audience breathing space in a longer presentation. Avoid talking heads where possible. There's no point in trying to make your presentation interesting if you're then going to have a boring video presentation in the middle of it.

Stand and deliver

Unless you are delivering the budget, a prepared statement or other detailed information, you should try not to read your presentation. Nobody asked you to give a reading – they wanted a presentation.

Ideally, you will talk directly to your audience without the benefit of notes. This takes considerable practice and confidence and, therefore, you should normally try to talk directly to your audience using prompt cards (with the main messages in bullet points). Your slides should also give you a logical narrative to guide you.

When you're very confident in yourself and your material you can leave the lectern and stand center stage. But don't be in a hurry to do this – the lectern is very useful for confidence and for resting notes on.

Practice what you preach

Before the day, do your presentation to someone else. Tell them to stop you whenever they don't understand something. Simplify and clarify anything that is misunderstood. When you're speaking aloud, if you find you have to pause for breath in any particular sentence, then that sentence is **too long**.

Rehearse until you are comfortable and familiar with the whole structure. If you're stumbling over a particular bit or it doesn't seem to flow, change it.

Whoa there!

If you are using a microphone, make sure it's at the right height for you to stand up straight. Talk to your selected audience as if you were in a large meeting room. Project but don't shout. Let your voice tell the story just as you would to a friend. Your delivery will be more conversational and you'll sound more genuine.

When you first begin to talk, try to slow down your speaking pace. This will give you a chance to flush adrenaline out of your system. It also gives your audience more time to settle down and begin to listen. Vary your pace. Pause after major points, and look up at your audience, as if to say 'Did you get that?' Even if you are apprehensive, look happy. Relax, and your audience will relax with you.

Always look your audience in the eye, and that means picking out individuals and looking them in the eye. Good eye contact will help you control and involve the audience and allow you to get their feedback.

Taking questions

At the beginning of your presentation, make it clear how you want to deal with questions. With smaller audiences it is generally a good idea to allow clarification questions during the presentation and general questions afterwards.

Prepare for the questions as much as you prepare for the speech. With a bit of thought you will be able to anticipate what the most likely lines of enquiry are going to be.

Questions come in three sorts:

◆ requests for clarification

◆ requests for more information

◆ opinions.

Listen carefully to the balance between information given and information requested. Questions will always tell you what the person is thinking. Address their issues before you get back to your own.

Don't rush to answer questions. A pause makes it look as though the questioner has asked a really good question and gives you time to think.

Finally …

Never say 'finally …' in a presentation unless you are within two minutes of finishing. If you say it two or more times the irritation level of your audience will increase dramatically – especially if you are being followed by coffee, lunch or the bar.

Always check whether your presentation will benefit by reference to what has come before and what will come after.

When you think you've finished preparing your presentation, ask yourself once again, 'What is it I really want to say?' and check to make sure your presentation actually says it.

And remember the 6Ps: Proper Preparation Prevents Piss Poor Performance.

Relax and enjoy it.

doing

innervation

momentum

Written communication

HOW TO SAY WHAT YOU HAVE TO SAY ON ONE SHEET OF A4
(Give the big message in the headline.)

Background (or Brief)

Business people are hungry for information but they don't have time to consume it. In the new economy, people won't have the time or inclination to read long-winded, over-written reports. The executive summary is all anybody wants. Business writing is about holding up thoughts long enough to get someone else interested in them.

My view/reasoning/rationale/viewpoint/proposal

The secret of business communication is brevity, organization and clarity. Written communication therefore needs to be organized to give the maximum possible information, in the clearest possible way.

Support (or why we believe this, or our approach)

1 Brevity

Write in headlines. Decide what your most important message is and start with that. If you haven't got an important message then you haven't done your work properly. Keep your supporting facts and figures separate – if people want them they can find them but they shouldn't hide the main message.

2 Organization

Organize your information the way it is organized on this page.

◆ Start with the background, i.e., the history or context of the assignment.

◆ Then give your viewpoint. This is what you're paid for, so say something useful.

◆ List the supporting points. Don't be afraid to list contrary points and deal with them.

◆ Conclude by repeating your main argument and suggest actions: who does what when.

3 Clarity

In business, it's best to be single-minded. You can't say everything at once but make sure you say something. Don't use the passive. Say, 'I believe' or 'I recommend'. Take responsibility. Don't write like a civil servant.

A good way of structuring your thoughts is OPINION + FACT + REASON + EXAMPLE

I believe we should eat more fruit. Fruit is vital to a balanced diet. It's full of vitamins and minerals. A single orange gives all the vitamin C a healthy adult requires in one day.

Actions (next steps or recommendations)

◆ Make a copy of this today.

◆ Use it as a template for your own business writing.

◆ Study other documents to see how they're structured.

◆ Only use one side of letter-sized paper from now on.

making things happen that you want to happen

As Jack Welch may have said at the beginning of this book, there are three kinds of people in the world:

◆ those who make things happen;

◆ those who watch things happen;

◆ those who wonder what happened.

There has never been a better time for those who want to make something happen to actually go out and make it happen. That's one of the beauties of the new economy.

However, it's still quite easy to forget that work is actually intended to have a result and that the reason why we work is to achieve something and generally make something better.

In the new economy, things happen faster. The pace of change has accelerated. Not all of that change is controlled and not all of that change is necessarily beneficial to you. In the turbulent waters of the new economy you will be washed away if you don't know how to paddle your own canoe.

There are certain disciplines required to get things done. Many of these are as old as the hills; some are particularly relevant to the new economy where the old levers of power are redundant.

Before we get to these rules, it's worth spending a bit of time examining the business environment. Business books tend to deal in a Utopian world where strategies are executed, marketing people know about adding value, finance directors can add up, leaders lead, workers work. That's not the real world, that's Germany.

What 'business-like' really means

People who have very little experience of office life, like vicars and pet show organizers, sometimes say that they want things to be 'business-like'. Those of us who are actually in business know that 'business-like' tends to mean a series of escalating cock ups relieved only by miraculous last-minute escapes and heart-stopping close shaves.

Everyone promises in business, few deliver. (Which is a step forward from the bad old days when no one promised and no one delivered.) The main reason for this is that nothing in business is simple or reliable.

Never trust someone in business who says something will be 'as easy as ABC' – he probably can't write. Similarly, 'pieces of cake' tend to contain nuts which cause a nasty reaction to anyone who attempts to eat one; a 'walk in the park' generally becomes a late night mugging with huge loss of money; 'falling off a log' ends up with you underneath the log and the rest of the tree; 'run of the mill' tends to be a sawmill with one of your legs each side of it; 'a piece of piss', you get the idea.

The three things that conspire against business on a daily basis are human error, mechanical breakdown and acts of God.

These are, of course, interrelated in that mechanical breakdown is generally the result of human error, human error is the result of acts of God and acts of God, on closer inspection, generally tend to be mechanical breakdown. At a deeper level, there are human breakdowns, acts of machine and errors of God which all make for really spectacular cock ups.

At the peak of the unreliability curve is the human being. Give someone an order and he will mishear it, misunderstand it, do the wrong thing in the wrong way and deliver it to the wrong person at the wrong time in the wrong place. Ask someone to come to a meeting and he will get the wrong place on the wrong day, with the wrong end of the stick, and during the meeting his ignorance of the subject will be matched only by the vehemence of his opinions on it. The one thing you can absolutely rely on in business is unreliability. That's what 'business-like' really means. If you want 100 per cent efficiency, call in the vicars and pet show organizers.

Why any form of change is so difficult

Given the fact that most people are working incredibly hard, it's amazing how little gets done. That's because however hard you work, there are always powerful forces working equally hard against you. Chief amongst these is something called 'process cheese'. This is a combination of bureaucracy, stupidity and inertia and traditionally forms the main strata of every company in much the same way that mozzarella forms the main strata of most pizzas. Trying to change something in business is like trying to cut a clean piece of pizza. It's impossible without pulling a whole load of stringy process cheese with you.

That's why you can't do something as simple as moving your pot plant without consulting widely, communicating internally, briefing your team, scoping the project, hiring consultants, preparing a budget and making sure everything is consistent with health, safety and environmental regulations, the company's mission statement and EU directives regarding transportation of agricultural products.

The second reason it's difficult to change anything is because everyone is scared stiff of the risk involved. As we've said before, risk can mean failure leading directly to written warnings, firing, unemployment, eviction, marital breakdown, family break-up, impotence, alcoholism, madness, drug addiction and death. So when you suggest a minor improvement in the stationery ordering system, don't be surprised when people see you as a bringer of destruction and death.

If you actually manage to get something done, don't relax and get all complacent. In business it is a cast iron rule that whatever you are empowered to do, your boss is empowered to undo. It also follows that the longer it takes you to do something, the quicker your boss can undo it. If you're doing a project that represents your life's work, it's a good idea to make sure you're not reliant on the sign-off of someone who suffers from intermittent post-lunch tetchiness.

The biggest impediment to change at work is something called the committee stage. This is like the Wells Fargo stage in that it generally gets ambushed by hostile forces with completely different agendas. Committees gather people together who know nothing about a subject, allow a five-minute briefing on a three-year project, and then expect to generate an intelligent response when most minds in the room are focused on how heavy the demand is going to be for the pink wafer on the biscuit plate.

Changing things – how not to do it

Every so often at work you decide things have got to change. Anything can trigger this feeling:

◆ suddenly realizing you've been in a temporary job for 20 years;

◆ finding an urgent memo addressed to you by someone who has been dead and buried for three years; or

◆ the growing awareness that your job description reads like a rehabilitation program for the criminally insane.

Once you're gripped by this feeling, you very rapidly decide that enough is enough. Those of a violent disposition would, at this stage, go out and destroy a bus stop.

The rest of us start doing a number of things that we wouldn't normally do.

The first thing you do is clear the decks for immediate action by slicing the end off your rubber, untangling your telephone cord and putting 90 per cent of your paperwork in the bin.

You then clear up your computer by reorganizing all your files into an easy-to-use, logical system that divides everything into three folders: Work, General and Other. For the first time since you joined the company you decide to empty the wastebasket on your computer and free up two-thirds of the memory. You get into this so much that you accidentally throw away all your major applications and the company's main server.

Having completely cleared your computer you then tackle your in-tray. You work incredibly hard for three hours without even looking up and do a month's work, including all the really nasty things that you've been putting off for years, like customer service. After that you phone people you don't like in the office and say 'no' to their stupid, time-wasting ideas. When you've got that off your chest you then make a neat list of all the things you're going to do to really get you into the fast lane of life, like learning German, getting an MBA and cutting back on the ice cream. Finally, you decide that this sort of efficiency means it's high time you had a new, high-powered job, so you register with an executive placement agency.

By this time your burst of energy is beginning to fade and you move into the smug and content phase where you admire your empty desk, your clean rubber and your empty in-tray. This phase very rapidly becomes the extended lunching and shopping wind-down period, where you handsomely reward yourself for being so good.

Once you finally get back in the office, you spend what's left of the afternoon telling everyone how hard you've worked and catching up with your social calls, interrupted only by the executive placement agency calling you back to offer you the superb job opportunity of the person two promotions beneath you. At the end of the day you go home still smug enough to justify the following four weeks of utter and complete idleness at work.

The four ways to succeed in business

1 Do nothing and succeed

You would have thought that lazy people would form an inert mass at the bottom of an organization. On the contrary, they are found at all levels in business, right up to chairman. The reason for this is simple: when something goes wrong in business it's generally because someone somewhere has tried to do something. Obviously, if you don't do anything, you can't be blamed when it goes wrong. People who sit all day like a lemon busily straightening paperclips are therefore the only people with a 100 per cent record of success, and with that sort of record the world is your oyster.

In business these days, we are all encouraged to work smarter not harder. This ignores the fact that there is a hard core of people who don't work smart or hard – in fact they hardly work at all. They are the 'motivationally challenged', traditionally known as lazy sods, and every office has at least one of them.

Strangely, lazy sods are always the busiest people in the office. Whenever you ask them to do anything there is no way they can help because they are far, far too busy. If you ever get irritated and ask them exactly what it is that they're so busy doing, they will have a long list of things that sound devilishly important. The truth is, if you'd asked them the same question a year previously, the list of things would have been exactly the same.

Lazy people actually lead very full lives because they take an ass-achingly long time to do simple things like photocopying. In order to fill their days, they use a special technique, the exact opposite of prioritizing, by which they unerringly select the most trivially unimportant aspect of a job and devote their entire energy, if not their whole working life, to it. For example, they will spend two days looking for a first-class stamp to make sure your post gets delivered as soon as possible.

The only time lazy people show any signs of activity is in meetings held to discuss more efficient working.

doing

innervation

momentum

Suddenly, they're bursting with all manner of schemes and innovations all of which, sadly, they are far too busy to implement. However, they're happy to have as many meetings as you like, because to them meetings are just like being down the pub – a nice relaxing chat until it's time to go home.

If you have to work with a lazy person you have two options:

◆ you can either ask them to do a job, remind them, re-remind them, cajole them, plead with them, threaten them, get eaten up with stress, have a nervous breakdown, see your marriage break up, drift into alcoholism and drug abuse and finally end up down and out in Swindon; or

◆ you can do the job yourself.

There's only one downside to the lazy person's attitude and that is once every three years consultants come in and ask everyone what they do. Those people who say 'nothing' are then made redundant (outside the company rather than inside).

In the transparent new economy it's very easy to see who is adding value and who isn't. Therefore option one is not an option for success.

2 Do something useless, move on quickly and succeed

Traditionally, to get ahead in business you need to be the sort of person who is seen to be doing things. Of course, everyone is doing something, namely their job. Therefore, people who do something over and above their normal job are noticed and get promoted. From this derives the curse of modern office life – the initiative.

An initiative is born when it gets a name. Your job doesn't have a name therefore it is not an initiative. But invent something called the Parallax Project or Vision 2010 or Raising our Pants and you have an initiative. There are only six types of initiatives: quality, cost control, empowerment, innovation, team working, and customer service. These come around as perennially as daffodils and once you've been through a whole cycle it's probably best to leave the company before your cynicism becomes a threat to the entire organization.

You don't have to be creative to have an initiative, that's what consultancies are for.

They are experts in creating the biggest possible deal out of the smallest possible idea and finishing up with the largest possible invoice. They have drawers full of original ideas tailor-made for your company.

All initiatives must include the following:

◆ a ring binder of worksheets which are jargon-free, interactive and fit neatly on the top shelf;

◆ a printed mousemat to show just how easy it all is to understand;

◆ a launch conference where everybody interacts and understands during the day and drinks and forgets during the evening.

Initiatives are always described in the same way:

◆ It's a revolution not evolution (or evolution not revolution).

◆ It's more than just an initiative, it's going to become the way we do business.

◆ It requires everyone's involvement and has the personal endorsement of senior management.

◆ It involves a step change in performance to put us up where we belong which is simply the best.

The way to manage an initiative is:

◆ Rubbish all previous work.

◆ Start the initiative and over-promise results.

◆ Hire consultants with big reputations.

◆ Blow the budget.

◆ Take the credit.

◆ Move on quickly before it all goes pear shaped.

◆ Blame someone else.

doing

innervation

momentum

Changing anything in business is a victory in itself. If the change is big enough and you're quick enough you can claim a vast amount of credit before the magnitude of the disaster becomes apparent.

In any large organization there are lots of initiatives going on at any one time. Therefore, your initiative can be to blow the whistle on any one of these ongoing initiatives as being a pointless waste of time and money. Everyone will rapidly agree with you and you will get all sorts of bonus points for being so tough and rigorous and single-minded.

In the new economy, the business cycle has shortened. Nobody's going to have an initiative called Vision 2010 because by then the company may well have disappeared or changed completely. The only 'initiatives' that will be undertaken will be directly plugged into the market and will be measured there.

3 Do something and succeed

You decide to do something, you execute it, it succeeds, you benefit. Theoretically this can happen so it's worth trying. But read the next way just in case.

4 Do something, fail, learn, adapt, try again, fail, learn, adapt, try again, fail, learn, adapt, try again, fail, learn, adapt, try again and succeed

When you attempt new things you may make mistakes. The trick is to learn from your mistakes. This makes you grow and mature as a person. If you don't learn you just look increasingly stupid. Also, you don't want to just keep learning otherwise you'll end up with so many lessons you'll become a business guru – which is someone who knows a hell of a lot about business but doesn't actually have one.

Keeping out of the workhouse

Most people who've achieved anything worthwhile in life or business have done it the fourth way. A few people have the luck of the devil and just have to put their hands out in a high breeze for money, fortune and everything else to blow directly into it. Unfortunately, these individuals get a lot of publicity and give the false impression that success in anything doesn't require a monstrous amount of effort.

If you are trying and trying again, you may or may not succeed but really you've already succeeded. That's because life can be divided into those who make the effort and those who can't be bothered. When you're old and gray (in your early forties in other words) you'll look back and all that matters is that you tried. You gave it your best shot.

In the new economy, where you are increasingly on your own, there's not much institutional momentum to keep people going who aren't trying. It's like a sieve. Those who manage themselves and motivate themselves will keep their independence of mind, imagination and spirit. Those who don't will end up in jobs that are constantly supervised and monitored. These places may have modern lighting and pot plants but in effect they are the new workhouses.

Live and learn

Learning has become a bit of a cliché in business terms (God knows I've banged on about it enough) so it's worth revisiting what we actually mean by it. First, if you don't do anything you won't learn. Second, there's generally a gap between your expectation of what would happen and what did happen. Third, you understand the reason for the gap. Fourth, you try again in a different way, incorporating the lesson learned.

This definition of learning underpins one of the most effective learning organizations in the modern world – the US Army. It has a special center for lessons learned. The sole purpose of this is to make sure that lessons learned the hard way (especially for those in combat) are disseminated across all its armies around the world within minutes.

The building block of this system is something the US Army calls the AAR – the After Action Review. It's disgustingly simple and frighteningly effective.

After every engagement or exercise the team leader conducts the AAR. There is a rule that AARs mustn't take more than 30 minutes max.

You'll notice there isn't any part of the process for bitter recrimination and dishing out the blame. AARs are all about learning the lesson quickly and then moving on.

In essence, this replicates the engine of evolution where all progress and evolution is through mutation. Mutation is where something has gone slightly wrong, some physical feature or behavior is slightly different from the norm and actually improves performance. Over time, through more successful breeding, this feature becomes the new norm until the next successful mutation.

Business evolution is also through mutation so you therefore need to protect your mutant people and ideas.

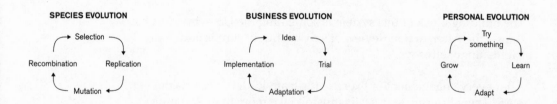

| SPECIES EVOLUTION | BUSINESS EVOLUTION | PERSONAL EVOLUTION |

What happens when things don't happen

Learning in life and business isn't always as neat as AARs. Sometimes your business may fail or you find yourself in the wrong job. It's likely, in the new economy, that these two things will happen more frequently. There will be no more jobs for life and many more people will be attempting to do things and build new businesses on their own.

Here's how to resign and move on effectively and with the least possible stress.

How to resign effectively

◆ Resignation is a strategy not a tactic

◆ If you want to shout, do it outside

◆ When you're calm make the decision

◆ If it feels right at 9am, it is right

◆ Carry on working happily

◆ Look for a new and better job

◆ Complete all paperwork

◆ Resign gracefully and thank everyone

◆ Try to avoid working your notice

◆ Take time between jobs if possible

Customer service is all in the imagination

The one thing that you have to do in business is to 'make it happen' for your customers. Sadly, when people start talking about customers, they stop talking sense.

Customers are just like you and me.

So before we start talking about serving customers let's ditch some of the clichés.

Legendary customer service

It's like the legend of the Holy Grail. Everyone's heard of it but nobody's seen it.

Delighting the customer

The British people don't do delight except on two occasions: the successful completion of a world war or the birth of a puppy. Customer service just doesn't do it for us.

Exceeding customers' expectations

I don't know about you, but when I go shopping I expect the worst – the last thing I want is someone to exceed my expectations.

Having an obsession with the customer

What does this mean? Do you follow customers everywhere, go through their dustbins and leave weird notes under their windscreen wipers? If my local butcher was obsessed with me as a customer, I would think twice about asking for a Cumberland sausage.

The customer is king

Apart from getting the sex of 50 per cent of your customer base wrong, most people in life don't think of themselves much higher than eight of clubs.

The customer is always right

Most people aren't right about anything else in life so why should they suddenly become omnipotent when they go shopping?

Customers only know three things:

◆ They know what they like.

◆ They know it when they see it.

◆ They know whose money it is.

They don't want to be right. More than anything they want us to be right. They want us to have the right products, at the right price, delivered at the right time, in the right way.

So don't ask the customer about the future – ask yourself.

Markets are about imagination not customer research – imagination in developing products and services and imagination in applying them to customer needs. If you want to own the future you have to invent the future.

Imagination is more powerful than knowledge.

Einstein

doing

How to make it happen for customers

◆ Don't keep them waiting

◆ Act on their feedback

◆ Let them choose their channel

◆ Deliver when you promise

◆ Keep them informed

◆ Make paperwork clear and easy

◆ Involve them in development

◆ Never compromise on quality

◆ Make doing business a pleasure

◆ Treat your staff as well as customers

innovation

momentum

working with other people not as talented or good looking as yourself

'Hell is other people.' That's what John Paul Sartre said. But remember he was French.

Nevertheless, he does have a point in that many problems in business come from people and the many excuses they find for not getting on with each other. In the new economy, where personal relationships are key, knowing how to manage people, to work with people and to put them at their ease are all absolutely core skills.

River crossing

Let me tell you a story. It's a very simple story and after you've read it, I'm going to ask you some questions. So if you're sitting comfortably …

Once upon a time there was a man and there was a woman and they were very much in love. All they wanted to do in life was to be together. Sadly, they couldn't be together because they were separated by a deep and fast-flowing river. The only way across the river was by a ferry. The woman spoke to the ferryman and said, 'Will you take me across the river? My true love is on the other side and I long to be with him.'

The ferryman replied, 'Of course I will take you over the river. Simply pay me the fare and jump aboard.' To this the woman could only reply, 'I'm afraid I have no money, but I'm desperately in love and I long to be with the man I love.' The ferryman shook his head, 'If you have no money, then you can't use the ferry.'

Suddenly, a stranger appeared who had happened to overhear their conversation. He took the woman aside and said, 'I hear you have a problem. If you make love to me I will give you the money for the ferry and you can be reunited with the man you love.' The woman agreed to his proposition. They made love, she took the money and was able to pay the ferryman to take her across the river. On the other side of the river she was reunited with the man she loved and they all lived happily ever afterwards.

Or they would have done were it not for a friend of the man who happened to cross the river the very next day. He heard from the ferryman what the woman had done to pay her fare. When he met his friend, he told him what his true love had done with the stranger in order to pay the ferryman. As soon as the man heard what the woman had done he confronted her and said, 'I know what you did yesterday and I never want to see you again.'

The questions you now have to answer are:

◆ Who do you think behaved best?

◆ Who do you think behaved worst?

Try to put your answers in order. Best behaved at the top, worst behaved at the bottom. There are no right or wrong answers. Just decide what you think.

Finished?

Not easy was it.

The really interesting thing about the story is how people react to it. In a group of approximately 20 people there will always be somebody who thinks that every one of the characters behaved worst and somebody else who thinks they behaved best.

Here are the rationales they come up with to explain their choices.

Man in Love

Best: He had principles and he felt the woman had betrayed these principles. He took a firm line based on strong beliefs.

Worst: He made no attempt to listen or understand the actions of the woman he was supposed to have loved.

Woman in Love

Best: She was prepared to make any sacrifice for love.

Worst: She had the morals of an alley cat.

Ferryman

Best: He was just doing his job. Why should he take someone across just because they were in love?

Worst: He had no compassion and would not help a woman clearly in distress.

Stranger

Best: He provided the solution to the river crossing problem. He was clearly a natural facilitator.

Worst: He took advantage of a vulnerable and desperate woman.

Friend

Best: He was a good friend and was prepared to tell the truth to protect his friend.

Worst: Had he kept his mouth shut they would have lived happily ever after.

The one moral that can be safely drawn from this little story is that every one of the characters believed he or she was doing the right thing for the right reasons. When people hear this story, some people can see what they believe to be the right actions for the right reasons. Others see the wrong actions for the wrong reasons. Or perhaps they see the wrong actions for the right reasons.

Life is very much like this story, not in the river crossing aspect, but in the people aspect. Often you come across people who seem to be doing the wrong things for the wrong reasons. Instinctively, you tend to put this down to them doing the wrong thing through stupidity, ignorance or malice.

And no doubt they think the same about you. A very important piece of rewiring is to allow yourself to believe that other people are trying to do their best with the best intent. If you can suspend judgement for a moment you can begin to understand their personal goals and motivations. In doing so, you illuminate more clearly your own goals and ways of achieving them.

People in the old economy

Many companies claim proudly, generally in their mission statements, that people are their most important asset. If you wanted to get a mortgage and you said that your only asset was your people you would end up living in a tent. Again, beware companies that say with great sincerity that they are a 'people business'.

Roughly translated this means they are in the slave trade.

If they're not in the slave trade then perhaps they mean that they are a people business to differentiate them from a racoon business. And if they don't mean that either then perhaps what they mean is that they are in the meaningless platitude business or, as it is more often referred to, management consultancy.

It should (but doesn't) go without saying that all businesses are run by people for people. When you've knocked around for a bit, you'll know that there are really no business problems, only people problems. That's why everyone would be absolutely delighted with their jobs if it weren't for the people involved. Traditionally, the way to deal with people is in exactly the same way as you do in normal everyday life: completely ignore them unless they get in your way or they want to give you money.

doing

innervation

momentum

Very often people who work in an office say that all they want is to be treated like a human being. This is usually said by people who are being bullied, ignored and generally abused by a management that are all, with the possible exception of the Finance Director, human beings. They would be better served if instead of asking to be treated like human beings they asked to be treated like a can of baked beans. In this way they could guarantee that every care would be taken in their initial selection, they would be in a protected and temperature controlled environment, they would be continually promoted and would bring satisfaction to customers everywhere.

If you want to work for a company that really looks after you, avoid ones that have a lot of big talk about 'people'. They will be as concerned with people in the same way that people's republics are concerned with people. There is one test and one test only for a company that really values its staff: if the company does well you benefit, and if you do well the company benefits. And in the old economy you can count companies like that on two hands and a foot.

In the new economy people will want to do business with people they like. So if you want to be 'nice people to do business with' you better make sure you hire nice people to do business with. However, in the new economy where the pool of talent is more fluid and fast-flowing than ever before, competition for good people will be so intense that the way you treat your talent will be as important as the way you treat your customers.

So how do you do it?

How to manage people

Establish mutual expectations from the start

People don't need to be controlled if they're going in the right direction and doing the right thing in the first place. They only need to be controlled when they're not doing what's expected of them.

Deciding what you expect of someone and what they expect of you in any given situation is the best form of controlling and managing that situation. As long as you set the mutual expectations before you start anything.

If I expect you to call me every day, you know exactly how to keep me happy. You also know that I will be unhappy if that doesn't happen and once you fail to call me every day I can point out that we both agreed on this point and something must have changed for you to be failing to live up to our expectations. You can't complain that you didn't know I was expecting a daily call because we've already agreed what's expected.

Clearly agreed mutual expectations worked out in advance go a long way to mitigating the worst effects of that business bugbear – bad communication.

Monitor working relationships while they still work

Things can go wrong in business and relationships deteriorate. Like marriages they have to be worked on and it's best to do the work long before it's really needed. The rule with relationships in the new economy is that if it ain't broke, service it.

When affection for you is the only thing that separates you or your brand from the competition in the mind of the consumer, you better make damn sure that you keep in contact, that you say the right things and that you listen for any minute changes in wants, needs or expectations.

Put people at their ease

All human relations go more smoothly when the people involved are relaxed. Being relaxed is a function of not being threatened by anything so when you want somebody to be relaxed you must make sure nothing about you – your posture, your message, your rank, etc. – is threatening.

It is a real gift to be able to make total strangers feel at ease because naturally we're all wary of strangers. Smiling, listening, self-deprecation and a pinch of flattery are the keys, and people who can employ these at will are said to be charming. Charm is a great word from the last century which suggests some kind of oil-based preparation in the hair, but charm is the ultimate business facilitator. As someone rather charming once said:

Charm is getting the answer yes before you've even asked the question.

(Could have been Jack Welch but doesn't sound like it.)

doing

innervation

momentum

With people we work with over a period of time, familiarity encourages relaxation, but people need to be re-charmed every time you meet them. You know you've got a friend rather than a business relationship when you've banked enough of this relaxation and charm to be able to be a grumpy old sod with them once in a while.

The fastest way to put someone at ease is to make them feel superior. You can do this by admitting you're stupid or sad or unlucky. But the fastest way by far is to bang your head quite hard against a low beam. This instantly robs you of dignity, composure and intelligence and makes virtually anybody else look as though they've got their life together. This approach isn't recommended for important business meetings.

Don't take people for granted – thank them now

The most efficient way to get something done in the office is to have said thank you to everybody the last time. If you're the sort of person who dumps on people at the last moment, screams for results and then doesn't give a word of thanks, you'll find it gets increasingly difficult to get anything done, because everyone will glue your stuff to the bottom of their in-tray.

It won't help your case either if the first time you've bothered to speak to them is when you're dumping a massive amount of work on them. You need to have put in the spade work a long time before.

Manage in context – understand all sides

In the old economy of command and control companies with hierarchical structures, the pattern of management was very easy. It went downwards and kept going down until it reached the bottom.

Nowadays, matrix management, relationship management, virtual management, and upward management are some of the models you can choose for managing relationships with other people. It's no longer enough to know who is above and below you in an organization, to work effectively with a person you have to have a clear idea of the context in which they are working.

One of the oldest mistakes in the book is to have a meeting with a few people and to focus on the person you consider to be the most senior.

The new economy doesn't work like that. You have to understand as quickly as possible the shape of the other person's role: their point of saliency or where they add most value in their team.

There is a little trick for finding out what it is: asking and then listening.

Ask people what they think about things

The most sincere form of flattery is to give someone your undivided attention. This gives them a very clear signal that you think they are worth listening to. Most people actually have strong opinions about how they could do their job better and how you could work together better. Most people are also deeply wary that they won't be listened to and that their opinions are of no account.

Very often if you ask someone about their job and how they do it, you will learn something of use for the way you do your job and also for the way you can work more effectively with that person. Plus the very act of listening and acting on what you've heard is a powerful cement for your relationship.

Be aware, however, that there are a sizeable number of people who don't think but do like to talk, which they assume is the same thing. These people have one or two opinions which they've worked hard at, polished up and relish the opportunity to trot out. Occasionally, take a deep breath and give them the opportunity to do so, but try to have an exit strategy on hand in case they are on a continuous loop and start repeating everything.

Avoid upsetting people

Thousands of books have been written about interpersonal relationships and how to get on with your loved ones. Now that everyone is completely happy at home, someone ought to pay attention to office relationships. You will often hear people blaming political or communication difficulties when something goes wrong at work. Boiled down, all this means is that someone, somewhere has been upset.

The quickest way to upset someone in the office is not to value their work. So when they've prepared a 50-minute presentation, ask them to do it in five; or get together a working party on their specialist subject and don't include them; or have a team celebration and don't include them because their job is so basic they don't really count; or ask them to do something and then tell them how to do it in minute detail; or ask them for some extra work and then don't use it; or ask them why their job hasn't been done away with yet.

The lower you go down the office hierarchy, the easier it is to upset people. If your job is to push a button you're not going to take kindly to anyone who tells you where, when and how to push it. Only those people who respect your absolute mastery of button pushing or form filling or barrier lifting will be allowed to benefit from a display of the aforesaid mastery.

The only sure-fire way of getting people to help you is to follow this tried and tested formula: get to know them before you need them; ask someone's advice on their particular job; remember their name; respect their time; listen; and then thank them sincerely.

Go for lunch – you can't bond with a sandwich

Lunching has all the benefits of a meeting without any of the drawbacks. It's also something people enjoy doing and there's an additional benefit, in that you get proper food (see *Lunch* in *Be Your Own Boss*).

Stay calm and keep a sense of humor – it's only work

Business can get very stressful at times and it is during these times that people's behavior tends to deteriorate; they get snappy, they stop listening and they start panicking.

It's the measure of the quality of a person how well they react under pressure. When you're staring a deadline or some other nasty in the face, this is precisely the time when you must keep your head, steady other people and think clearly.

The best way of keeping this frame of mind is to keep things in perspective. At the end of the day (and the day will end however unpleasant it is) you're not at war, your family isn't at risk, you're not about to die. If you're going to look back and laugh at something, you might just as well laugh at it now.

How to manage people

◆ Establish mutual expectations from the start

◆ Monitor working relationships while they still work

◆ Put people at their ease

◆ Don't take people for granted – thank them now

◆ Manage in context – understand all sides

◆ Ask people what they think about things

◆ Avoid upsetting people

◆ Go for lunch – you can't bond with a sandwich

◆ Stay calm and keep a sense of humor – it's only work

How to get people to change

In an ideal world we would all have mutually understood expectations, we would all stick to them and we would all be happy.

The reason we are not in an ideal world is because expectations are rarely mutual, often misunderstood and generally not stuck to.

Which is why to get things done you'll often require someone to change their behavior. In the old command and control economy you would command them to change and control their behavior by having their genitals in a vice.

Things work rather differently in the new economy. People have much more liberty and inclination to do their own thing in their own way and therefore getting them to change their behavior requires a new technique based on getting them to want to make the changes for their own benefit.

And remember, you're not trying to change the person, you're only trying to change their behavior.

Start with some praise for the person

When people are threatened they tense up, they get all rigid (physically and mentally) and the likelihood of them changing of their own accord is zero.

Step number one therefore is to put them at their ease and make them relaxed. Praise for their work does this, but again it's no use suddenly appearing out of the blue and telling someone they've got the wisdom of Solomon, the looks of Leonardo di Caprio and that you've always admired their work (unless you're trying to get Leo to do something for you).

Mention your own mistakes in the area

Human beings can sniff out an implied criticism at one hundred paces. There's also the fact that blaming other people is most people's default option as far as self-criticism goes. Combine these two facts and you'll understand how carefully you have to tread to avoid apportioning of blame or finger pointing.

You can totally disarm someone by starting, 'I think I've made a mistake, and I need your help to get me out of it.' This gives them the triple whammy of not being criticized or blamed, being asked to help and also the satisfaction of knowing that you've made a mistake.

Of course, we know that your mistake was choosing to work with this person in the first place, or not agreeing expectations, or not checking in with them that things were going according to plan. But for their benefit this is presented as a mistake in understanding what they were doing, how hard it was, etc.

Talk about the effects of their old behavior

Talking about the effects of their behavior removes them from direct criticism and blame while highlighting that it might not be the right behavior for the desired end. Once you can agree that you're not getting the right effects, it's a short and fairly easy step to work out what the causes are and how they can be changed (as long as you don't jump in with blame and the pointing finger).

Understand the reasons for their old behavior

Generally, in business, people are doing what they believe to be the right thing for the right reason. Understanding why they are doing what they are doing is generally a good short cut to changing what they do. They're either under constraints that you don't know about or have other priorities that you don't know about. Once you understand these you can manage and change their behavior more easily.

Explain the benefits of new behavior

You, no doubt, will be aware of the benefits of what you want them to do. Before you ask them to change, make sure that you have identified some clear benefits for them in changing their behavior. After all, self-interest is the most powerful motivator.

The other side of the coin is ensuring that the changes of behavior imply no loss of face or diminution in status for the person involved. Would you want to do what you're asking that person to do?

Tell them the change is well within their capabilities

Any kind of change is a potential threat to people, so you need to reassure them that the change is well within their capabilities. If it isn't then you need to make sure you give them the appropriate support every step of the way. Also it makes sense to have the first part of the change the easiest so they don't find the transition too daunting.

You can't teach a man anything, you can only help him discover it within himself.

Galileo

While we're on the subject of astronomy, it's worth remembering that everyone thinks that they are the center of their own universe and not in orbit round your sun.

Agree targets for changed behavior

Finally, when people understand why the new behavior is needed, what the desired effects are and what the benefits to them and everyone else are, you need to complete the circle and agree expectations about their role, behavior and actions.

doing

innervation

momentum

When the new behavior is emerging, you need to continually monitor and encourage the behavior and make sure the power of old habits doesn't re-emerge.

Give them a new title and job description

Some people just do what's expected of them. Often with these people, the fastest way of changing their behavior is to change their role, their job description and their key measurements.

How to get people to change

◆ Start with some praise for the person

◆ Mention your own mistakes in the area

◆ Talk about the effects of their old behavior

◆ Understand the reasons for their old behavior

◆ Explain the benefits of new behavior

◆ Tell them the change is well within their capabilities

◆ Agree targets for changed behavior

◆ Give them a new title and job description

do less, earn more

Everyone who's been in business more than five minutes will know that they have to work smarter not harder. If you run a factory there are pretty straightforward ways of doing this. But what about individuals in the new economy? The trick is to be more effective and more efficient.

There is a difference between being efficient and being effective in business. Being *effective* means that the effort you put in has the right effect; in other words you get what you want. Being *efficient* means you put in less effort to get the same effect. You can get what you want by working yourself to death but you'll be a lot happier all round if you also work efficiently.

How to be efficient in business

Get organized before you get an organizer

Working smarter not harder doesn't mean the application of more and better technology. It is more important that you yourself work efficiently. Before you get a personal organizer get yourself personally organized. If you're clear in your own mind what is useful, important and what is mission critical data, then you can cut a clear swathe through the information clutter that surrounds us all.

Start work half an hour earlier

It's easy to think that by working later at the office you give yourself permission to start work later. In reality, that is not how it works. Once you start getting late in the day, it has a knock-on effect and you find yourself losing more and more time during the day. Starting early, on the other hand, gets you ahead of the game and makes it easier for you to stay ahead. Remember, it's always easier to prepare for a meeting before it than after it.

Work in small digestible chunks

There is a very popular postcard somewhere that says something like, 'I'm fascinated by work, I could sit and look at it for hours.' That may refer to boring, uninvolving, repetitive work. But the situation is more serious when you have so much work you don't know where to start. You don't know where to start, so you don't get started. The longer you leave it, the harder it is to start and pretty soon you've got a major psychological block.

Instead remember that even the longest journey starts with a single step. Explorers crossing the Antarctic never think of how far it is to the other side. They concentrate simply on the next ten yards. Get started and then concentrate on keeping moving one block at a time.

Think in the morning, act after lunch

Most people think better in the morning. Mental activity certainly goes down after lunch, especially when it's been a three-course lunch with a bottle of wine. At the same time, most people's jobs are a combination of thinking and doing. It stands to reason that you should think in the morning when your mind is fresh and do things in the afternoon when you don't need your brains for processing power. But resist the temptation to ditch lunch, which is a powerful business tool.

Put time for you in your diary

Keep control of your own diary. Especially resist the urge to fill all your own white spaces. If you're nervous about opening your diary in front of friends or colleagues and for them to get snow blindness because your days are so empty, then just fill them in with all the things you're going to think about. Add a name and the time and everyone will think you've got back-to-back meetings (the Holy Grail of the traditional economy and recipe for ulcers and general unhappiness). Don't put things in your diary unless they absolutely have to go in.

Only travel if you'll return richer or wiser

It's very easy to write 'meeting in Doncaster' in your diary when it's five weeks away. Five weeks later you realize that Doncaster is a hell of a long way away (unless you live in Doncaster) and it will take almost all your waking hours to get to the one meeting. Unless you're really desperate to see somewhere without paying for it, don't waste time travelling. A good measure of whether time spent travelling is time well spent is to ask yourself whether you will return richer (in money or spirit).

If you're not adding value, delegate

If you've got a dog, don't bark yourself. If you're in a team, let the rest of the team members do their jobs. If you're a team leader, let everyone do the jobs you've asked them to do. In your own job, make sure you're spending your time and effort on adding value. Do what you do best and give the rest to people who do it better than you do.

Plan tomorrow but act today

Get started now. Problems and tasks are always easier once you've got started. A good place to start is with the planning: who is going to do what by when. Business crises are often avoidable given a little bit of planning and foresight.

How to be efficient in business

◆ Get organized before you get an organizer

◆ Start work half an hour earlier

◆ Work in small digestible chunks

◆ Think in the morning, act after lunch

◆ Put time for you in your diary

◆ Only travel if you'll return richer or wiser

◆ If you're not adding value, delegate

◆ Plan tomorrow but act today

How to be effective in business

Define your goals and stick to them

Without a set of goals and a clear direction in your work, you're never going to know whether you're working effectively or not. Without clear goals you won't know when to say 'yes' to opportunities and when to say 'no' to work that is irrelevant.

As you work your goals may shift. This is because working and gaining knowledge and experience often illuminates and defines your goals more clearly. It's not necessarily a sign of weakness if you change your goals either. Over the course of life your goals change naturally, the key thing is to feel some sort of purpose and direction to what you're doing.

What you must avoid doing is ditching your goals as soon as the going becomes tough. All the good things in life and the things worth doing are difficult to achieve. They require the continuous application of intelligent and directed effort. Unless of course you've made your goal just to pick the low-hanging fruit of life. Just be aware that a lot of other people also take the same approach and there is a limited amount of low-hanging fruit. (When I used to pick blackberries with my father, he said to avoid the low ones as dogs peed on them. I'm sure there's a lesson there.)

Be enthusiastic – it's contagious

In business, the difference between people who become directors of large companies (their own or others) and those who don't often boils down to nothing more exciting than confidence: the confidence in their own abilities and the corresponding confidence they inspire in others.

Confidence is actually more important than ability. There are many examples in business of people whose supreme self-belief has carried them unscathed from one monstrous cock up to another. They get away

doing

innervation

momentum

with this because their confidence is so rock solid that they simply can't believe that any mistakes could possibly be anything to do with them. Similarly, all their shareholders and employees believe the same.

Confidence in yourself and your beliefs can be communicated in two ways: arrogance or enthusiasm. Arrogance means you see yourself as better than other people; enthusiasm means you want to share the good news with other people. Arrogance may help you with weak people who lack confidence in themselves. In their uncertainty, they will latch onto the arrogant as being sources of strength and uncertainty, and there are all sorts of examples of the arrogant leading the weak, from cult leaders to Hitler.

On the brighter side, an ounce of enthusiasm can go a very long way in business where cynicism and despair are widespread and are sometimes even touted as business virtues. Deep in the heart of the most jaded, bitter business person, there is a strong desire to have something to believe in and to work for. They won't find it in company mission statements, but they will recognize it in individuals fired with enthusiasm.

Life in general is a lot like a sponsored bike ride. People will go out of their way to back people with enthusiasm, especially for a cause that seems well-founded and well-thought-out. And don't forget, enthusiasm doesn't mean talking in tongues and emitting a strange aura of light: it means communicating to others that you are happy and inspired by something worth doing and that they would also be a help and inspiration to you.

Talk to people with experience

Arrogant people don't talk to people with experience because they worship at the altar of their own intelligence. Intelligent people do talk to people with experience because it's a fantastic way of learning about and avoiding big pitfalls.

When you talk to people with experience (see *Networking*) you're not just listening to what they have to say, you're also telling them what you have to say and gaining supporters along the way. Remember, people are generally happy to help, they just need to be asked.

However, when you're listening to people with experience you should only listen with one ear open. That's because everyone's experience is different and what worked yesterday won't work tomorrow. Also, people with experience are talking from memory, and the memory is a very efficient PR department, creating myths and polishing the truth so that over the years, events and decisions become almost unrecognizable.

Take short-term pain for long-term gain

As we said above, everything worth doing has a large cost attached in terms of time, money and effort. Therefore everything worth doing requires an investment of time, money and effort. It's this investment which we define as pain. Why? Because it hurts. Working really hard for a long time hurts. Investing a lot of money in something hurts, especially when you haven't got a lot of money. Investing money is a risk and the psychological strain of risk can be every bit as difficult as long-term hard labor.

Naturally, there's always a no pain route. You always have a choice to do it the easy way. If you want the no pain, big gain route you can win the lottery or be a bastard and succeed. Sadly for you, short-term gain normally has long-term pain attached to it.

The only really safe way to avoid pain is to go for the no pain, no gain route although this usually amounts to no pain, no gain, no life.

Do it, then talk about it

If talking was the same as doing then the world would be a strange and dangerous place. In the business world no commodity is cheaper or more freely available than talk. At the other end of the spectrum, no commodity is more valuable or harder to come by than effective, targeted and profitable action. Anyone can talk about doing something, very few people actually do something. Academics have a phrase for this: 'Money talks, bullshit walks.' Money here is used as an abstraction of effective action.

When you go through life, it's useful to have a mental bullshit detector on at all times. Traditionally, some phrases in life have always scored a very high bullshit factor.

HIGH BULLSHIT FACTOR	LOW BULLSHIT FACTOR
The check's in the mail	Remittance advice
You can have some equity	Share certificate
I'm writing a novel	Book
It's a successful e-business	Dividend
You have my support	You have my money
Two-way communication is important	What do you think?
I love you	I'll change the diaper
Market leader	Market share
We must have a meeting	Let's put something in the diary
I'm going to set up my own business	Here's my card
I was just going to call you, Brian	Great to hear from you, John

Under-promise and over-deliver

Everything in life is relative. If I ask you out for dinner at a restaurant and we go for a kebab, then you're likely to think I've over-promised and under-delivered, your bullshit detector will register a very high reading and our working relationship will have been damaged.

If I've promised you a kebab (not a recommended business practice) and take you for a slap-up feed in the Manoir de L'Addition Grand then I will have under-promised and over-delivered and our business relationship will be strengthened.

The point is that everyone judges results by their expectation of results. If you're the favorite and you come second, you've done badly. If you're a no-hoper and you come second, you've done well.

In the new economy, where so many business contacts are service relationships, the trick is to set manageable expectations of delivery.

These should always err on the cautious without being uncompetitive.

You don't want to use under-promising like the railways use it: making journey times ever longer in the timetables in order to cover weaker and weaker performance. Instead you want to set expectations at a level where they can be met 80 to 90 per cent of the time, with the final 10 to 20 per cent of times exceeding expectations.

This gives you the double benefit of always being seen to deliver on target and often to be delivering above and beyond targets. Over-promise and you will consistently fail to meet the target and often be way below it.

When you're ready, take the big risk

Life doesn't happen one little step after another. Sometimes it requires a long, running jump into darkness. It sounds scary and it is scary. So scary in fact that many people choose never to make that leap of faith and rather continue their one little step after another even though it's leading them away from opportunity and fulfillment.

Now that doesn't mean you have to go hurling yourself into the void every five minutes. People who do this spend most of their lives in intensive care, or receivership as it is sometimes known.

As we know, the real risk in the new economy is to take no risks at all. Taking no risks means you're not innovating and moving forward, and if you're not moving forward, someone will catch you up and before you can start moving you'll be road kill on the information superhighway.

There are two types of risks in business: calculated and harebrained. Harebrained you won't need any coaching for. Calculated risks mean understanding the exact nature of the risk and doing everything in your power to mitigate it.

doing

innervation

momentum

When you're making a leap into the dark it would be nice to know certain things:

◆ How long your run up is.

◆ How wide the gap is.

◆ How fast you'll need to run to get over the gap.

◆ What's on the other side.

One out of four is the most you can expect. Any more and it wouldn't be a risk. What you can do is to prepare your run up as much as possible, i.e., applying time, effort and resources to giving you speed and momentum in the required direction. Once you're actually mid-jump or mid-risk you'll probably begin to see your landing site. It may not be what you anticipated but it certainly won't be anything like the place you've left.

If it is a recognizable place then you have failed to achieve what NASA calls escape velocity, the speed needed to escape the pull of earth's gravity.

Even when you have taken the big risk and landed somewhere you didn't anticipate, you still have something working in your favor whatever the location and that is the power of momentum. A famous army general who wishes to remain nameless (I can't remember his name) said, 'With momentum I can achieve anything.'

This was the principle of Blitzkrieg in the Second World War: that with sufficient speed, aggression and energy, any obstacles can be overcome.

When you're ready to take a risk and have achieved escape velocity, anything is possible.

The harder you fall, the harder you become

Henry Ford said that, 'Failure is the opportunity to begin again more intelligently.' We all know this now, even though it doesn't make the sting of failing any less painful. Failure doesn't just teach you about the project in hand, it also teaches you about yourself.

At the beginning of her book *Damage*, Josephine Hart, says, 'Damaged people are dangerous, they know they can survive.' This is the bleak version of failure, which can be translated more optimistically as 'People who have met disappointment know it's not the end of the world and just crack on to the next thing.'

While we are in the mood for quotations, Rudyard Kipling said:

If you can meet with Triumph and Disaster and treat those two imposters just the same …

Rudyard Kipling never recovered from the death of his son in the First World War and we shouldn't really confuse deep personal tragedies that damage human beings with business setbacks that cause a few sleepless nights and the loss of a few dollars.

Focusing on what's really important in life will put the shallower business triumphs and disasters in their proper place.

'No' is a diversion not a stop sign

On a micro level 'no' is like a small business disaster. It means you have failed to get your own way.

People say 'no' for all sorts of reasons. Generally, because they haven't got the time or money to support you, or because they believe what you're doing is wrong. Just because someone says 'no' this doesn't mean that your project is not worth time or money or that it is wrong. 'No' is only one person's opinion. You can either ask someone else or take the reasons behind the 'no' and change your project for the better.

In the long term, the only 'no' you really have to worry about is from your customers. When customers say 'no' that really is the last word.

Never get personal unless it is personal

Occasionally people will say 'no' to you because they are a bastard and because they can't stand other people showing the initiative and confidence that they sorely lack.

The natural temptation here is to wreak bloody and awful vengeance on them. Don't. It's inevitable that throughout life you will meet

doing

innervation

momentum

people who don't like you and don't want to help you. In normal life you can just avoid these people and be on your way. In business you often can't avoid them; they may well be your boss.

There are ways to manage this situation (see *Managing Your Boss* and *Managing Bastards*). But the one road you don't want to go down is making it personal. As soon as you make it personal for them, you make it personal for you and you allow the places which matter to you, such as your dignity, self-respect, confidence, happiness, to be exposed to their attack. You give them power to affect all these things. As hard as it may seem, you must do everything in your power to treat these people in a professional manner.

Very, very occasionally, even in our caring, sharing, coaching new economy, you will find yourself in a position where the personal and malicious actions of another individual threaten your livelihood and, by extension, your nearest and dearest. You then have two options. Remove yourself and start somewhere else, or confront the problem personally. Once you have taken this second course you have to strike

---

How to be effective in business

◆ Define your goals and stick to them

◆ Be enthusiastic – it's contagious

◆ Talk to people with experience

◆ Take short-term pain for long-term gain

◆ Do it, then talk about it

◆ Under-promise and over-deliver

◆ When you're ready, take the big risk

◆ The harder you fall, the harder you become

◆ 'No' is a diversion not a stop sign

◆ Never get personal unless it is personal

hard, strike quickly and sustain the attack until your opponent is rendered completely harmless. Generally, you'll be dealing with bullies and if you show bullies any weakness they will exploit it.

Changing the way you work

There are four ways people think about changing the way they work:

◆ chucking it all in for an alternative lifestyle

◆ starting your own business

◆ working from home

◆ making more money.

Let's look at them in order of probability. The most unlikely option first.

Chucking it all in for an alternative lifestyle

They say that the grass is greener on the other side of the hill. Whoever 'they' are, they're talking rubbish because, given the choice, very few people opt for the scorched brown side of the hill in the first place. So when you're sitting quietly at your computer screen in the IT department and you think that life would be much better out in the country building dry stone walls, think again.

And if when you've thought again, you still think it's a good idea, sit yourself down and give yourself a damn good talking to, because you may think it's a good idea but dry stone wall builders up and down the country know it's a fantastically bad idea and they would give their right arm to be where you are now had they not already lost it in a horrific quarrying incident.

Excessive media attention is given to people who have downshifted and simplified their life. It's too good a story to mention the fact that they've actually taken early retirement on a pension five times the average wage. If your average office worker attempted to downshift, they would very rapidly find themselves living in a compost heap whittling turnips into owls for craft fairs. And if you're going to end up doing that, you might just as well stay in IT.

You can actually completely change the important things in life by changing aspects of what you're already doing.

Starting your own business

The myth about starting your own business is that you work for yourself. You don't, you work for other people. If you really want to work for yourself, join a multinational company where you can happily work away for 40 years with no noticeable effect.

Many stressed, aggressive people who work in big companies leave to start up their own businesses where they are totally dependent on stressed, aggressive customers in big companies.

Setting up a business isn't about being your own boss, it's about being your own office junior, your own receptionist, your own marketing, sales, IT and finance director. Only do it when you have a really good idea and you absolutely want to rather than doing it because you have no idea what to do and you absolutely have to.

Working from home

Sometimes a long commute and a hard day at the office can be too much to cope with. That's why there is a growing trend towards downshifting. This is a way of re-balancing your life by reducing stress at work and spending more time at home with your family.

Sadly, you may find that time spent with your family is actually the cause of stress. If a survey was done at three o'clock in the morning when your screaming baby had just woken you up for the third time, the result would be 90 per cent of executives desperate to spend less time with their families and more time in the office.

When you work from home you have to be rigidly disciplined in separating business and pleasure. In the morning you must throw off your duvet, walk through into a separate, dedicated office and then settle down under a much more formal business duvet.

The downside of working at home is that you miss the buzz of the office because, let's face it, listening to a sneezing guinea pig is no match for a good gossip with Hayley on reception, although both have the same business value.

The alarming thing about home working is that you can do an entire day's work in 12 minutes. What's even more alarming is the number of other things you can find to do first. These are things you would never dream of doing at home normally, such as re-corrugating the shed or rodding the drains as a precautionary measure.

Working from home will increase in the new economy. However, this will mean one or two hours a day or perhaps one or two days a week. Bosses will have less of a problem allowing people to work at home if they are in constant contact by phone and e-mail. At the same time, people who have the choice of where they work will value the office for the social and community aspects of it.

Making more money

Companies often have mission statements stuck up on the wall explaining why they're in business. If their employees had their own mission statements on the wall, most of them would say, 'I need the money.' Of course if someone paid you a nice salary to lie in bed all day picking your navel then we'd all be lawyers.

Money talks and what it usually says is 'spend me.' The reason why people work a five-day week and have a two-day weekend is that you can generally spend money twice as fast as you make it.

A great many working people only go to work to earn money so that they can pay the bills, look after their family and have a couple of holidays a year. If you are not one of these people and you derive a certain amount of satisfaction from what you do, then you are one of the lucky ones.

The difference between a business book and any other book (and the reason why they sometimes cost that little bit extra) is that somewhere, in amongst the rubbish, there's got to be something that will help the reader make more money.

It's amazing just how many business books and how many businesses are shy about money.

Often they will avoid mentioning it all together. They will talk about shareholder value or value added or margin. But what they're really talking about is money.

Money. Money. Money. Money. Money. Money. Money. Money.
Money. Money. Money. Money. Money. Money. Money. Money.
Money. Money. Money. Money. Money. Money. Money. Money.
Money. Money. Money. Money. Money. Money. Money. Money.
Money. Money. Money. Money. Money. Money. Money. Money.
Money. Money. Money. Money. Money. Money. Money. Money.

Feels a bit embarrassing seeing it all there doesn't it.

But there's nothing dirty about money. It's an abstraction of abundance. Profit is when we get a return on effort. It's the bedrock of all civilizations. Without money there would be no art, no architecture, no hospitals, no schools, no emergency services, no cathedrals, no roads, no peanut butter, no nothing. Money makes the world go round and people who think otherwise are the worst kind of flat-earthers.

Love of money, on the other hand, is no good for anyone because money has no intrinsic value. Wanting money for its own sake is a shortcut to missing everything that's truly valuable in life like love, family, community, compassion, adventure, education, faith, laughter, Morris dancing, etc.

So clearly there has to be some kind of balance.

Let's assume that you're a normal working person who wants to make more money, not because you're a moneygrubber, but because you want to facilitate more of the good things in life. So how do you make more money? Everyone knows really, they just keep forgetting and hoping they'll win the lottery. Just to remind you, here are the golden rules.

1 Do what you do best and ditch the rest

Everyone has something they can do well. Keep focusing your job so that a greater and greater proportion of it comprises what you do best. Then concentrate on doing your thing better than anybody else.

2 Charge on value not cost

Understand the worth of what you do rather than its cost and then charge accordingly. Remember the worth of something is decided by the people who buy it (this explains how modern artists make a living).

3 Improve your skills

Keep training and learning and getting qualifications until the point where people don't quite understand your CV. A potential employer shouldn't be able to read your CV and say, 'Monkeys could do that.' A skill is defined not just by what you can do but also by what others can't do.

4 Cut costs that aren't useful or enjoyable

None of us wants to be the grim-faced killjoy from the accounts department, but once you look at what your costs are, it's amazing how and where your money drains away. On the other hand, if you think you're going to save your business by charging staff for their tea and coffee or getting them to lick their own stamps, you probably don't understand business or people.

5 Stop adding and start multiplying

They say that if you look after the pennies, the pounds will look after themselves. Don't believe it. All you'll end up with is dirty fingers and a sack full of coppers. Look after the pounds and you can stuff the pennies. If you keeping thinking of a 5 per cent pay rise, you may well get it, but you'll also be satisfied with it. You need to decide that you want to be paid double what you're currently earning. Then you'll start thinking of how that can be achieved and that will require bigger and bolder moves.

doing

innervation

momentum

6 Keep changing things

Things will change even if you don't change things yourself. So if it ain't broke, fix it anyway. If you stand still in business you'll be run over. It's not the big who eat the small, it's the fast who eat the slow.

7 Make sure effort is linked to reward

Get performance related pay and then perform. Whether it's piece rate or share options, you need to benefit directly from your own labor (but remember that people work harder when the work's worth doing).

8 Change your job

If you earn a salary, the quickest way to increase it is by changing company. When your company can't do without you, it may be time to do without them. Having the courage to move on is a sure sign that you're ready for something bigger and better.

9 Take control then take ownership

If you really want to make a wallet-bending amount of cash, you really need to own the company or a substantial part of it. The first step to doing that is to take ownership of your own actions. Nobody's going to give you control over anything until you have full control over yourself.

10 Build a business to meet an unsensed want

Give people what they never knew they wanted. People don't buy what they already do, know or have, so sell them something they haven't done, can't do, don't know or don't have. Best of all, sell them something which they've never even dreamed of but which you have. And sell it in a language they understand, in a package they find attractive and at a price they will pay.

11 Either be a lawyer or strenuously avoid them

If you know you want to earn money and you don't really care how, then you should find yourself a job in a sector which pays a lot of money such as the law, management consultancy or financial services. Alternatively, try to avoid putting yourself in a situation where you ever have to pay any of their exorbitant daily rates.

12 Always get a better quote

We live in a free market economy which means everyone competes to deliver goods and services. Having said that, it's amazing just how few people bother to get another quote, or put something out to tender. Or even negotiate on a single offered price. The first price you're offered for anything always has some slack in it. Unless you're shopping for fruit and vegetables and then you'll just annoy the greengrocer.

13 Chase debtors to hell and back

They're stealing your money. Treat them like the criminals they are.

14 Work harder, faster and smarter

Now this one may come as a bit of a shock to some people. But normally you get rewarded for effort. Today, in our fairly meritocratic, open society, and for the first time in history, the harder you work the richer you get. And, again for the first time in history, the well-off are likely to work a lot harder than the badly-off. Very few people working a 35-hour week are paying top rate tax.

This doesn't mean you have to work a 60-hour week to earn more money. You have to concentrate all your time and effort on doing those things that earn you money and cut out everything else which is a waste of time, energy and money.

doing

innervation

momentum

How to make more money – the golden rules

◆ Do what you do best and ditch the rest

◆ Charge on value not cost

◆ Improve your skills

◆ Cut costs that aren't useful or enjoyable

◆ Stop adding and start multiplying

◆ Keep changing things

◆ Make sure effort is linked to reward

◆ Change your job

◆ Take control then take ownership

◆ Build a business to meet an unsensed want

◆ Either be a lawyer or strenuously avoid them

◆ Always get a better quote

◆ Chase debtors to hell and back

◆ Work harder, faster and smarter

I guarantee that none of these rules will come as a surprise to you. They're all easy to write down, difficult to live out.

Finally, bear in mind that making money isn't everything and that you can have just as much fun making other things such as music, sheds, love and pancakes. The things to ask yourself are:

◆ What exactly are you going to do with the extra money?

◆ What do you really want out of life?

◆ What kind of person do you really want to be?

Which leads us back to the beginning of this book …

We must not cease from exploration. And the end of all our
exploring will be to arrive where we began and to know the
place for the first time.

T.S. Eliot, *part-time poet, full-time banker*

doing

innervation

momentum